W9-AZY-795

Veils

BEYOND *the* TORN CURTAIN

CINDY BLOCKSIDGE ∬ RANDY HARDY

Veils: Beyond the Torn Curtain

Copyright © 2011 Cindy Blocksidge and Randy Hardy

First Printing, September 2011

All Scripture quotations, unless otherwise indicated, are taken from the *New Revised Standard Version Bible,* copyright 1989, Division of Christian Education of the National Council of the Churches of Christ in the United States of America. Used by permission. All rights reserved.

Scripture quotations marked NIV are from the *Holy Bible, New International Version* © 1973, 1978, 1984 by the International Bible Society. Used by permission of Zondervan. All rights reserved.

All rights reserved. Except for brief quotations embodied in critical articles and reviews, no part of this book may be used or reproduced in any manner whatsoever without written permission.

Printed in the United States of America.

ISBN 978-0-9838562-0-7

To order visit: *www.myveils.com*

*This book, purely and simply,
is dedicated to God.*

But when one turns to the Lord,
the veil is removed.

Now the Lord is the Spirit,
and where the Spirit of the Lord is,
there is freedom.

2 Corinthians 3:16–17

CONTENTS

Acknowledgments

Writing *Veils: Beyond the Torn Curtain* was a joy for both of us. There is no question that we had help from a lot of people along the way!

First and foremost, we need to express our deepest thanks to our spouses, Russ and Susan, for saying "yes" when we initially asked for their blessing upon our desire to write a book. Their continued blessing upon this project helped sustain our efforts, especially when leisure time we spent writing and editing may have occasionally intersected with "their" time.

Next, our appreciation goes out to our families. They have inspired and motivated us in ways that they may not fully realize. To our kids—Luke, Lisa, Jake, and Sam, as well as their spouses and the grandkids—we hope you all know that we celebrate *Veils* with you. We did it...realized a dream and wrote a book! We encourage each one of you to pursue your own dreams and then to follow through on them!

To the Sunday school classes and various small groups at McEachern Memorial United Methodist Church, our home church, who went through the *Veils* pilot classes when the manuscript was still a work in progress, we want to thank you so much for your honest insights, opinions, thoughts, and prayers. There are also several people we affectionately called our "readers." They read and reread our raw material and helped us by gently offering their feedback and ideas. We truly appreciate each one of you— you know who you are!

To the editing, layout, and graphic design professionals who helped guide us and direct us—and kept us from accepting merely "good" as the highest achievable level— thank you for pushing us to exceed our fundamental goal and to produce a book that glorifies God, will help other people, and is written with excellence! So, to Cynthia Lanning, Michael Dowling, and Amy Braswell, we have such high regard for each of you and appreciate all of your contributions.

Finally, we both know with certainty that we are beyond blessed because God has allowed each of these people to be a part of our lives.

Thank You and Blessings,

Cindy and Randy

INTRODUCTION

What images come to your mind when you hear the word "veil"? Perhaps you visualize the veil worn by a bride as she walks down the aisle, or maybe you picture the covering many Middle Eastern women wear to conceal their faces. A veil also hung more than two millennia ago in the Jewish temple to separate a sinful people from the presence of their holy God.

There are different types of veils. Some are opaque and others are semitransparent. They serve different purposes—to filter, partially conceal or separate. Whether we realize it or not, God has allowed us built-in veils to use along our life journeys. Equipped with these invisible tools, we develop ways to either filter or conceal ourselves and our emotions. We can choose to separate ourselves from others by veiling our true hearts from those to whom we are closest. Even though we cannot fully veil ourselves from God, we sometimes even

What images come to mind when you hear the word "veil"?

attempt to distance ourselves from God by not allowing a completely reciprocal, transparent relationship.

Our closets tend to contain far more veils than we actually need. Many of our personal veils do us a great disservice because they form barriers that separate us from experiencing fulfilled lives. However, there may be seasons in our lives when some veils are very helpful, too.

WE CHOOSE HOW WE USE OUR INVISIBLE VEILS

One reason we use our veils is because we don't want to expose ourselves to other people. Adam and Eve set the pattern in the Garden of Eden. They covered their nakedness with fig leaves in an attempt to hide their imperfections from God after realizing that they had forsaken him and abused their gift of free will. The separation between being human and being perfect, like God, became clear in the garden that day.

At times, God allows us to use veils for protection.

"Humanistic perfection" does not exist on Earth because only one person has ever lived a perfect life, and that is Jesus. Our calling is to surrender to God's perfection while we strive for our own. We get closest to perfection when we admit how far short we fall and thereafter seek to live Christ-like lives. But such humility is difficult for us, so we attempt to veil our humanness.

We also use veils to tame our fears. Frightened by the unseen and the unfamiliar, we pretend to be something we are not. Afraid to let others see who we really are, we construct an invisible fortress using all sorts of veils.

At times, God allows us to use veils for protection. These types of veils are useful at certain stages (or phases) of life and can actually prevent us from being self-destructive by keeping us from wandering into situations before we seriously and prayerfully consider the consequences. On the other hand, maintaining veils that no longer serve a purpose can imprison us. It is our job to discern which veils are useful and which ones are separating us from something good.

WHAT ARE YOUR VEILS?

What veils do you possess and have you maintained over the years? What invisible barriers do you hide behind? What parts of life are you filtering instead of allowing life to freely flow? *Is there a veil that can affect your relationship with God?*

Don't be surprised if you find these questions difficult to answer. Most of us are comfortable behind our veils. They've become so much a part of our identity and everyday lives that we're unaware of them. We barely know they exist because we're constantly using them and they are as familiar to us as the air we breathe.

Yes, some of our veils are sheer, like the veil over a bride's face. These veils are intended to filter and can actually balance our lives by pacing our actions *Is there a veil that can affect your relationship with God?* appropriately. Others are opaque, like the curtain that hid the powerful Wizard of Oz. These are intended to separate us from life's troubling situations during certain stages of life. We occasionally sense the presence of our veils, but we have trouble identifying them unless we intentionally look for them.

Do you identify with some (or all) of these veils?

Veil of Distraction
Veil of Complacency
Veil of Pride
Veil of Shortsightedness
Veil of Self-Reliance
Veil of Obsession
Veil of Choice

If any of these veils have caused your relationships with God, your spouse, family, friends, business associates or others to stagnate, please take the time to read this book. You will learn how to identify and understand your veils so that you can decide which ones to keep, which ones to modify, and which ones to discard.

Most of us are comfortable behind our veils. We barely know they exist ...

If you set your mind to it, with God's help you can overcome the veiled joy that may be separating you from a life of greater fulfillment. Most importantly, you can be the person God created you to be, if you modify or discard the veils that you no longer need!

Veils: Take a good look—God does!

1 ❙❙ DREAM IT – DO IT!

Veil of Distraction

Remember being a kid and lying on your back looking up at the sky? No pressures from work. No "real-life" challenges. Your parents and other grown-ups took care of those boring, big-picture things. You had more important matters to think about—and to discuss with an occasional friend who would join you—like what you wanted for Christmas and what that first kiss would feel like.

As children, we existed to play, eat, and go to school. Then we ate, played, went to sports or watched TV. On Sundays, we would eat, go to church, and play. In between eating and playing, sometimes we would . . . *Dream* . . . Most of the time, these were not the kind of dreams that we had at night when

> ❙❙ *At its best, dreaming is about communing with God, one on one.*

we were trying to run away from something and our legs wouldn't move or when we were falling and about to hit bottom. We were always glad to wake up from those kinds of dreams. No, these dreams were better, freer. They had to do with the shapes of clouds and the blue of the sky. These dreams were refreshing, like the smell of a summer rain storm or the feeling of fall just before cooler breezes robbed the trees of their vibrantly colored leaves—greens, reds, oranges, browns and yellows, all fluttering down like they had minds of their own.

Our dream sessions on a clear night were the best of all. As we gazed heavenward into the night's sky, we sensed the vastness of the universe. We saw an eerie darkness complimented by the beauty of the stars and moon and other planets. In these times God seemed to be so big, yet so close at the same time. Sometimes, we felt lonely. These were the nights that it felt really good to have a friend who would be dreaming beside us. On really, really special nights that friend would be of the opposite sex! On nights like that, we didn't want to hear our names being called to come home.

THE GOOD OLD DAYS, WHEN WE WERE KIDS

In the days before video games, cell phones and iPods, kids had more time to dream. Do you remember those days? Life used to be less structured and less complicated, didn't it? Kids in the "old days" hung around the neighborhood after school and played together. During the warm days of summer, boys and girls would play games outside from daylight to dark. They would get filthy dirty from rolling around in the grass or playing in the creek. They did not have to rush off to soccer practice or dancing lessons and this, that, and

In the days before video games and iPods, kids had more time to dream.

16

the other organized activity because their play was unstructured. Spontaneous play was the most fun!

When we were kids, we had more time to ask life's really important questions, too: *Does God live somewhere up there in the sky? How far up does God live? What does God do all day and night? Does God get tired of staying awake all the time? What does God eat; I wonder if God eats broccoli? Does God drink stuff,* too? *If so, does God prefer milk, water, maybe Diet Coke or— if he's a southern God—does he like sweet tea?*

Few of us "grown- ups" allow ourselves time to dream. Instead, we think.

As kids get a little older, the questions turn more serious. *Does God really love me like my Sunday school teacher says? How can someone I can't see love me? If God does love me, why does God let monsters hide under my bed? Why does God let my mom and dad fight, and why did he let my friend's parents split up? I hope my parents don't split up, like my friend's folks did.*

As adults, we realize that kids don't think much about taming their emotions, but they certainly are emotional, aren't they? Kids don't think much about responsibility either, but they are aware of what irresponsibility feels like. Kids have lots of questions about God because they don't fully understand God. However, as we grow older, we don't fully understand God either, do we? Kids certainly don't have a clue that God allowed them to have built-in veils meant to protect them and help them navigate through life. Yet, from an early age, we all use our veils to discern between right and wrong, as well as to shield us against some of life's challenges. Surely this is a sign of God's prevenient grace—the grace that comes before our acceptance or understanding of a relationship with God—directing us and also pulling us into God's arms of love.

Growing up—reality sets in

Dreaming is an important part of childhood, but then we grow up. Genesis 37:1–17 tells us Joseph dreamed as a

One significant barrier that blocks our dreams is the veil of distraction.

teenager. He didn't question his dreams and even shared them with his brothers and father. Joseph's dreams were insightful and revealed that he would one day rule over his family. But in his naiveté, he seemed to simply enjoy his dream and possibilities. Why, in the process of becoming adults, do we lose our capacity to dream? If we do not fully lose this ability, why does it wane? If we adults took time to dream, we'd see more clearly where we want to go and who we want to be. If we allowed ourselves more time to dream, we might once again become more aware of our personal needs, wants, and desires.

At its best, dreaming is about communing with God, one on one. If we spent more time seeking God's guidance, we'd make better choices about how to order our priorities and invest our time. We can see how important this kind of dreaming was to Solomon in 1 Kings 3:1–15. Solomon recognized God appearing to him in a dream and used that awareness to commune with God and seek his guidance. Solomon ultimately became a man known for his great wisdom due to his connectedness with God and his desire to discern and follow God's guidance.

It seems today that very few of us "grown-ups" allow ourselves time to dream. Instead, we *think*. We think about family responsibilities, vacation plans, losing weight, gaining weight, golf, football, shopping, sleeping, 401K plans, health, the stock market, college expenses, taxes, job security, a new car, a bigger home, going out to eat, keeping up with the Joneses, retirement, more football ...

You name it, we think about it! We analyze it, we worry about it, we pine for it, and we sometimes pray about it, too. But we don't spend much time dreaming—really dreaming—like we used to do as kids.

Like communing with God one on one, dreams won't usually happen in the midst of this day-to-day busyness unless we intentionally make the time to allow them to happen. We are so distracted these days, aren't we? So, one significant barrier that blocks our dreams is the *veil of distraction.* If we were more intentional about removing this veil, we would be freer to start really dreaming again!

Yes, dream time really is about allowing our minds to wander.

Think about this: What might happen if you exchanged some of your "think-time" for intentional "dream time"?

KIDS ARE A GREAT EXAMPLE FOR US

How as adults can we begin to relearn the art of dreaming? One way is to notice how very young children gaze curiously at the world through innocent eyes. See how they marvel at rainbows, at birds building nests, at flowers in bloom. Ask young children to describe the pot of gold at the end of the rainbow and they can do it! Why? Because they don't "think" as much as adults do! Kids are less distracted than adults. For children, becoming Miss America or Superman or anyone else is as easy as extending a dream to the next level. Children have much to teach us about what we've forgotten. Dreaming is essential because it opens our eyes to the opportunities God has for us that we might otherwise miss, if our *veil of distraction* (due to the busyness of life) remains in place. Take time to remember your childhood, when it was so easy and enjoyable to dream.

THE VACATION "DIVERSION"

The world in which we live is constantly changing. Our lives are like giant picture puzzles composed of innumerable moving parts. In this twenty-first century, every one of those pieces is moving at hypersonic speed. Most of us are so busy "doing" that we leave ourselves little to no time for really "dreaming."

Children have much to teach us about what we've forgotten.

Some adults do attempt a bit of dreaming when they're on vacation. Vacations are vitally important occasions to rest and relax with our spouses, children, and other family and friends. We need those respites of unstructured play so that we can let go of our jobs for a while.

But make no mistake: Vacation time is much different from dream time!

Vacations involve destinations, plans and agendas. They are, if we really think about it, yet another activity strategically planned to distract us from our everyday lives. Most of the time, we don't allow our minds to wander even while we are on vacation.

More often than not, vacations leave no time for dreaming. They're filled with sightseeing, amusement parks, swimming, sunbathing, and sports activities,

Can you dream about what life might look like if you were "still" more often?

shopping, dining out, sleeping in, and reconnecting with people we haven't seen in a while.

Without intentionality, dreams won't happen in everyday life or even on vacation because we are distracted.

In fact, sometimes vacations present big challenges because they offer additional distractions in unfamiliar surroundings. For example, Disney World is a magical place that came about because of one man's dreams that turned into a reality. But if you really think about it, going to the parks that Walt Disney built is not ideal for dreaming. After rushing to get there, we race to the gates to be first in line; then we rush from ride to ride while trying to read maps, eat ice cream cones, find bathrooms, strategize about how best to use our fast passes—all as we desperately try to keep the kids away from the gift shops until it's time to go home. From morning to late night, we walk, walk, and walk. Sure, it's fun and exciting, but there's usually no time left for dreaming while we are so busy distracting ourselves from our everyday lives!

The joy of a wandering mind

Dream time really is about allowing our minds to wander. It is also about seeking God's guidance concerning things we did not even fully know existed. It's about finding inspiration in stillness and listening to inaudible voices. Dreaming allows new ideas to stimulate our minds, new energy to refresh our bodies, and different perspectives to lift our spirits. When we put the everyday demands and responsibilities of life on hold, we seem to be more able to meet God at least half way, instead of excluding God from our lives. Have you ever been "so busy" or gotten so distracted that you could not find the time to commune with God or to dream about what God may want you to do for his kingdom?

When we allow time to dream, something wonderful happens—we open ourselves to God like we did when we were children. His inspiration prompts exploration; exploration stimulates imagination; imagina-

What if you did not allow distractions to interfere with your relationship with God?

tion gives birth to ideas; ideas lead to plans; and plans result in accomplishments. As we once more begin to dream and observe the benefits, we realize anew its importance. We can follow the life of Jacob throughout many chapters in Genesis. We see clearly his frivolity, self-reliance and even mischievousness in his childhood and youth. We see a different Jacob after God comes to him in his dreams; Jacob pays attention to his dreams and acts on them (see examples in Genesis 28:10–17 and 32:22–31).

Jacob's dreams became life-changing events as he felt God speak to him.

PLAN A DREAM VACATION

Are you willing to consider taking a vacation of a different kind this year—*a dream vacation*? Forget about passports, tickets, traveler's checks, and itineraries. Just leave your responsibilities and distractions behind and go somewhere to let your mind wander…as you did when you were younger.

> *At its best, dreaming is about communing with God, one on one.*

Before you "think" too much about what to pack on your dream vacation or get caught up analyzing your travel and meal plans, just ponder a few other questions first.

What would it be like if you were able to tear through your *veil of distraction?* As busy as you are, can you even imagine what a less-distracted life might look like? Can you dream about what a less-distracted relationship with your spouse or your family might look like? What would a friendship look like if it were less distracted? Can you visualize what your work environment might look like if you were less distracted by your coworkers or the needs of your boss? What if you distracted your coworkers less—would they be more productive?

Best of all—what if you did not allow so many of life's distractions to interfere with your relationship with God? Before you go on to the next chapter, reflect upon the familiar words of the psalmist in Psalm 46:10: "*Be still, and know that I am God!"* Can you dream about what your life might look like if you were "still" more often?

Take a good look at your veil of distraction—God does!

Parting Your Veil

1. Do you dream? If so, what do you dream about?

2. Think about the last time you had a daydream. What was it about? Describe it in your own words. What do you think it was telling you?

3. The authors state that vacation time is not the same thing as dream time. Do you agree? Why or why not?

4. Do you think that the *veil of distraction* keeps you from dreaming? What are some examples of distraction in your life?

5. What would your life look like if you were less distracted?

6. What would remove your *veil of distraction?*

2 ∬ MISSED OPPORTUNITIES

Veil of Complacency

We never see missed opportunities in our lives until it's too late. They come in many forms. From your own life, do you recognize or have you experienced any of these?

A business opportunity not seized
A relationship not pursued
A gift not given
An investment not purchased
A dream not acted upon
A friend not called
A change not made
A trip not taken
A kind word not spoken
A person not witnessed to

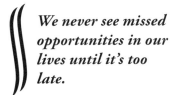

We never see missed opportunities in our lives until it's too late.

The list of life's missed opportunities could go on and on.

Missed opportunities can cost us money, cause us aggravation, create heartache, and hold us back from something important. But too often their causes are hidden from us by a *veil of complacency*, so we keep on missing them.

A FEW OF THE CAUSES

Think back over your life and recall one or more opportunities you missed. Adjust your rearview mirror until you can see them clearly. Now think back about your attitudes and actions at the time. Why did you fail to seize the day?

> *Opportunities are often hidden from us by a veil of complacency.*

If you're like most people, you can quickly give a variety of reasons. But look closer and you will probably find that most of your reasons are related to one (or more) of three root causes: *fear, money,* and *time.*

Fear is one reason people pass up opportunities. Initially folks become excited about a new venture. But once they begin addressing practical considerations, reality sets in, anxiety mounts, and enthusiasm fades; fear has allowed many an opportunity to fly by. Consider Pontius Pilate in Matthew 27:11–26. Was fear in the courtyard that day when Pilate had to decide which prisoner to release—Barabbas or Jesus? The people were shouting and demanding the release of Barabbas, a known criminal, rather than Jesus whom Pilate found had committed no crime. Did fear of the people drive Pilate's decision to release Barabbas instead of the man he knew to be innocent?

Money is another reason why people miss opportunities. Some don't think they have enough money. Others don't want to risk the money they have. And still others think an opportunity costs too much money. Matthew 19:16–26 tells us of the rich young ruler who just couldn't abandon his possessions to follow Jesus. That missed opportunity had eternal consequences!

Time is yet another reason for missing opportunities. People spend millions of dollars annually on books and seminars to learn how to better manage their time. But they may be looking at the wrong side of the coin. Instead of focusing on "time management," they should probably be addressing their "time mismanagement." We read in Luke 14:16–24 about guests who were invited to a great banquet. All of them had reasons that they could not attend. The bottom line was they had other things to do that took priority over the

> *Lack of faith can be overcome by placing trust in something that we can't see.*

dinner. They were all "too busy." They missed out on what was most important—communing with Jesus Christ at his heavenly banquet. We are all guilty of not properly ordering our priorities, thus mismanaging the time we are allowed.

The specific reason (or combination of reasons) for missing opportunities varies according to the personality and life circumstances of every individual. But fear, money, and time are by far the most common answers to the question, "What keeps you from *acting* on your dreams?"

A FEW OF THE CONSEQUENCES

Although everyone has dreams, and we all possess built-in veils to help us process a few dreams, only a few people act on them by removing their veils to make those dreams reality.

Veils: Beyond the Torn Curtain

In order to fulfill our visions, we should intentionally face (and try to overcome) barriers like fear, money, and time.

Business is an area where the *veil of complacency* commonly leads to missed opportunities. If you ask a businessperson why he or she failed to start a promising new business or participate in a lucrative venture opportunity, the answer will usually involve fear, money, or time.

Marriage is another opportunity that's often missed due to hesitations rooted in fear, money, or time. For instance, if you ask a young man why he keeps procrastinating about popping the question to the girl of his dreams, he may rattle off several "rational" reasons. But the root reason usually is fear: fear of the unknown or fear of commitment. Sometimes money is an issue too, but a young couple's concern about money may also indicate a fear of responsibility. Time can also be a factor, and it too can be linked to fear. A couple might be afraid that after they walk down the aisle and say "I do," they will regret exchanging *my* time for *our* time.

Yes, those two words "I do" sure DO change things!

(Yes, those two words "I do" sure DO change things!)

From the above examples of business and marriage, it may appear that fear, money, and time are major reasons why people don't pursue their dreams, desires, and visions. These are thought to be the principle veils that blind us and hold us back...or so it would seem.

But not so fast! Actually, fear, money, and time are not the primary reasons that people miss opportunities. They are only surface reasons that veil the root causes.

THE *REAL* CAUSES OF MISSED OPPORTUNITIES

The three underlying reasons (bigger-picture reasons than fear, money, and time) that keep most people from pursuing potential opportunities are:

1. **Lack of knowledge (don't know how)**
    and/or
2. **Lack of desire (don't want to)**
    and/or
3. **Lack of faith (don't believe in the unseen)**

If we really think about it, we realize that our *veil of complacency* can prevent us from seeing past our lack of knowledge, desire, or faith.

Although these obstacles may be monumental to some people and not so foreboding to others, the good news is that each of us can manage them in our own way and at our own pace to overcome them to the level desired. Sometimes we can overcome them by making relatively minor lifestyle adjustments, as follows:

1. *Lack of knowledge can be remedied by seeking more education.*
2. *Lack of desire can be overcome by nurturing our visions and displaying willpower.*
3. *Lack of faith can be overcome by placing trust in something that we can't see.*

All three of these actions work together if we will modify or drop our *veil of complacency.* For example, if we have the desire to do something, we can educate ourselves about how to do it. As we increase our knowledge and move forward, we find that our faith increases and we will naturally desire to do even more as we glimpse new possibilities.

God designed our brain and our heart to complement one another. God intentionally gives us a brain with which to think and a heart with which to feel. He designed our brain and our heart to complement one another. As our knowledge increases, we become more comfortable with our feelings. When we feel good about our decisions, we have more faith in their pending outcomes and ultimately we will become less complacent in the future.

Do you have trouble overcoming inertia? Are you a slow starter? Or do you start fast, but have difficulty staying on task and finishing well? Are you one who subscribes to the phrase "this is the way we have always done it" whenever you are asked to consider something different?

Whatever your shortcomings, you can overcome them in the area of desire. One way is to find an accountability partner who is strong in areas where you are weak. If you need motivation, for example, find a partner who will help you start your engine.

Some people who say they want to do things but just can't seem to get started may simply be lazy. The Bible calls them sluggards (Proverbs 6:6–11). Notice how desperate their lives become (v. 11). By observing others who are strong in areas where you are weak, you can gain motivation to overcome the veils that might be holding you back. Even a sluggard can be motivated.

RARE QUALITIES

Some people are natural born leaders and catalysts; they inspire us. The room seems to light up when they enter. Drawing on a reservoir of desire, knowledge, and faith, they always appear to be perfectly positioned to seize life's opportunities. Although these "competent" people are rare, you probably know a few. You may have read about some biblical characters who had these characteristics: Moses, Joshua, David, Lydia, Peter, Mary (who anointed Jesus' feet) and, of course, Jesus Christ, just to name a few.

What makes a person "competent"? To answer that question let's use an illustration from the construction industry. As you probably know, the government agency called OSHA (Occupational Safety and Health Administration) polices the industry to ensure that job sites and workers are safe. (Actually OSHA polices all types of industries, but most people identify OSHA as the "construction police.")

On each construction site, the OSHA representative will determine whether a supervisor is "competent."

What makes a person competent?

How does OSHA determine competency? It has nothing to do with race, gender, age, or national origin. OSHA doesn't care whether a supervisor was born in the North, the South, the East, or the West. People are *all* the same to OSHA; they are either competent or they are not.

To be considered competent by OSHA, the supervisor must possess only *two* things: *knowledge* and *authority*.

Either one alone is insufficient—"competency" requires both knowledge *and* authority.

Using the principles from this illustration and being as clear-minded as a conscientious OSHA investigator can you identify any competent people you have known? In your experience, who possesses both vast knowledge and unquestioned authority? Who appears to have more faith in the unknown than most other people? Who has the most desire? Do you know any community leaders, business owners, parents, teachers, clergy, family members, or friends who seem to be more "competent" than others?

You can increase your own competency by studying other competent people. Who are (or were) the most competent people in your life? What did they do to earn that status in your eyes? What would you say to them if you had a heart-to-heart talk today?

Competent people know that ignoring a *veil of complacency* results in stagnation. Instead of standing still, they figure out how to get things done. They also maintain faith in things that they cannot see, because they know that all of life's details are not pre-planned...no one but God can see everything coming and going.

A REMARKABLE STORY

We all know people who have amazing stories about overcoming obstacles to become the person that God created them to be. A typical story might go something like this:

> I grew up poor. Our family didn't have much of anything,
> at least not many tangible things. I and my six siblings

all worked on the farm. We got up each morning at 4:00 a.m. to tend the animals, and we went to bed right after sundown.

School was important, but survival was vital. That's why to this day I value every penny as if it might be my last. Growing up, our spaghetti hardly ever had meat in the sauce. We were satisfied with just butter and noodles.

One day I decided enough is enough. I promised myself that I'd do something more with my life. So when I turned eighteen, I went out on my own into the world. With $10.00 cash in my pocket and only the clothes on my back, I took off to grab at least a small piece of the "American dream."

> **Competent people know that ignoring a veil of complacency results in stagnation.**

The tenacity instilled by my family environment served me well. I possessed a burning desire to DO something with my life. I was attracted to the glitter and luxury of this very big, wide world, but I never lost my appreciation for the simple and honest life I had left behind on the farm.

I learned by the school of hard knocks that we are to love many, trust few, and always paddle our own canoe. With faith and determination, I educated myself. Then, I paddled my canoe vigorously until my life started to change. I paddled it right through the veils that had been holding me back and eventually realized the dreams that I had envisioned on the farm. In all of it, I never lost sight of my primary goals, which were to glorify God, help other people, and do everything with excellence. Yes, I have been very blessed in life.

Can you recall a real-life story that you have observed personally that looks and sounds like this story? Even though the details may differ, the theme will probably be similar. Most of us know at least one person who overcame limited resources and long odds to accomplish something significant. Along the way, he or she learned how to pierce the *veil of complacency* to get things done. People who gain the knowledge they need, cultivate their desire, and always keep their faith seem to prevail in life.

WORTHY OF ADMIRATION

Some of our nation's largest and most successful companies were started by "competent" people. Their stories inspire us. Nothing stopped them from saying "I want to do it" (desire) and "I will learn how to do it" (knowledge). Strengthened by an unshakable faith in the unseen, these people pressed on toward their personal goals until they attained them!

Maybe your "most competent" person did not start a company but did something else of importance or significance, at least in your eyes. We admire

There are competent people in every industry and walk of life.

people who have risen from their suppressed backgrounds to accomplish great things, both seen and unseen. Some have become college professors, medical doctors, hair dressers, nannies, engineers, construction workers, teachers, police officers, firefighters, stay-at-home moms, or scientists, just to name a few. In fact, there are competent people in every industry and walk of life.

When you think of people who you truly admire, who comes to your mind and what do they do? Are they tenacious and spirited people who had to overcome issues such as poverty, self-doubt, fear of failure, and numerous other obstacles? Maybe they did not let limited finances derail their dreams but instead recognized that money is simply a tool for getting things done. Perhaps they managed their time well and rightly ordered their priorities while drawing on the strengths of others.

What are the characteristics of the people in your life whom you most admire? Whatever they did in their personal journeys, somewhere along their

> *When you think of people you truly admire, who comes to your mind?*

journeys you can be sure that they tore through the *veil of complacency* that hindered them . . . and then they forged ahead. Their journeys may not have been easy, but they knew what they wanted and they went after it. We admire these people, and they deserve to be called competent!

THE ULTIMATE COMPETENT PERSON

We most admire the competent people who rise above all the others by not regarding their personal success as the finishing line. Rather, having successfully plowed their own fields, they intentionally look for opportunities to encourage others who are just reaching for the plow.

As you overcome some of the obstacles in your life by discarding some of the veils that are blocking opportunities, consider how you might share your knowledge and experiences to benefit others. When you help others shed veils that have kept them from realizing their potential, you are demonstrating unselfish love, just like Jesus did.

Take a good look at the veil of complacency—God does!

Parting Your Veil

1. What are some opportunities that you may have missed? What do you think is the main reason you didn't act on them?

2. The authors say that fear, money, and time are not the root reasons we don't "seize the day." Do you agree? Why or why not?

3. The authors state that the lack of knowledge, desire, and faith are root causes of missed opportunities. Do you agree? Of the three, what affects you the most?

4. What recent or current opportunity are you considering or have passed on? What is your response now, after reading this chapter?

5. Has the *veil of complacency* kept you from some opportunities in your life?

6. What do you think would happen if you lowered your *veil of complacency?* In what specific ways could you do this?

3 ⸾⸾ CHANGING PERSPECTIVES

Veil of Pride

Why are we so uncomfortable when we get caught changing our mind about a decision we've made or a direction we've chosen? Why do we have so much trouble "backing up" and rethinking our past positions? Could it be that we're afraid of appearing weak and indecisive, like politicians do when they "flip flop" on important issues, even when they change their minds because of new information? Maybe when we changed our position on some issue of our past, our pride was bruised because someone said "I told you so." Thereafter, we vowed to keep our mouths shut so that we would not expose our vulnerability again.

> *Rigidity in the face of changing circumstances is not strength; it's foolishness.*

Now, there's nothing weak about either holding firmly to fundamental convictions on the one hand or seeking new opportunities on the other. We should be rigidly committed to eternal truths and life covenants, even to the point of putting ourselves on the line for them. But rigidity in the face of changing circumstances is not strength; it's foolishness. By necessity we base our decisions on the information we have when we make them. When we gain a new perspective, many times it is wise to either adapt or amend past decisions.

We place the veil of pride between ourselves and other people.

The biblical story of Philemon (found in a brief book towards the end of the New Testament) is a great example of this principle. Apparently Philemon, a believer living in the city of Colosse, had no use for Onesimus, his worker, so he let him go. Onesimus may have even stolen from his employer. After the apostle Paul met Onesimus in another city and observed the changes that had occurred in his life, Paul sent Onesimus back to Colosse with a letter urging Philemon to rehire him. Paul was able to give Philemon a new perspective on his former employee.

WE BALK AT CHANGE

We are conditioned to believe that once we make a decision, we should stick to it *no matter what.* Because of this tendency, we often become proud and obstinate and place the *veil of pride* between ourselves and other people. When we make a decision to hold tightly to our deeply held beliefs and decisions regardless of changing circumstances or new information, we choose to be shortsighted (more about that in the next chapter).

Some of our decisions should be fluid and some should be unshakable. It is our job to decide which ones can change if needed and which ones are permanent. As you move along your life journey, circumstances will change, and thus your perspectives will change. You yourself will change too, due to the decisions you make. Realize and accept that sometimes you *should* change your mind. (Notice that we used the word "should" instead of "can," because although we all *can* change our minds, we don't always do it.)

The expression "hindsight is 20/20" is true, but we often do not look behind us because we are concentrating so hard on the future. When we look back at past decisions, however, we can actually discern the future ones more clearly. Sometimes we alter our future decisions using knowledge from lessons learned in the past. Even if circumstances make it impossible to alter a past decision, we can still learn from our past experiences so that we make better choices in the future.

> *Some decisions should be fluid and some should be unshakable.*

What was the hindsight perspective of Aaron and the Israelites after they became so prideful that they built and worshiped the golden calf rather than staying faithful to the leading of God through Moses, as described in Exodus 32:1–10? What did they learn that could help them make better future decisions?

DECISIONS WILL BE CRITIQUED

Recall a time when you made a decision and someone tried to change your mind (or your perspective). Were you so convinced that you were right about some subject or some past decision that you dug in your heels, pretending to listen to the other person's ideas but not really hearing them? Thinking back on that experience, why did you place that veil (perhaps it was more like a brick wall) between you and the other person? Was it your *veil of pride?* Were you told as a child that you should always stand by your decisions *no matter what?* Were you afraid to admit that you might be wrong? Do you have an inflexible personality? Does your skin crawl when others critique you?

Whatever the reasons, please consider one thing: Maybe your pride is the reason for some of your life's struggles and perhaps even caused you some conflicts. Very likely, it has prevented you from charting a better course along your life journey.

Let's look at the issue from another angle. Have you ever tried to change someone's mind about a decision, only to have that person place a *veil of pride* between the two of you? You might have offered valuable advice—maybe even an earth-shattering perspective that could have prevented a huge mistake—but the other person just wouldn't listen.

Does your skin crawl when others critique you?

How did you feel when the shoe was on the other foot? You'll probably agree that a *veil of pride* can hold you and others back. Many times, this veil is destructive because it can stifle advice that can prevent mistakes. We normally make decisions based on information we have at the time. Later when we gain more information, in hindsight, we may wish we had decided otherwise. How many times have you said to yourself: "If I had only known then what I know now"?

DECISIONS HAVE A RIPPLE EFFECT

Just like bare feet dangling in a pond's still waters, our decisions send ripples in every direction. Many times one decision propagates to affect others. Therefore, we can become afraid to make an initial change that might also change other things. But there can be other "ripples," too. When we make a change in a previous decision, we often need to tell other people we were wrong. To make matters worse, sometimes we make changes that affect others, too. Not only do we dislike admitting when we are wrong, we also dislike having to deal with the changes that come as a result of being wrong.

> *Just like bare feet dangling in a pond's still waters, our decisions send ripples in every direction.*

For example, what happens if you take a certain "dream job" and later decide you don't like it? You will have a choice to make: stick with the job you don't like or make a decision to change jobs.

But what if you had to move to another community to accept the job? You may need to make a series of minor life changes that affect you and your family. Your address, bank, dry cleaners, grocery store, doctors, and even your driver's license may have to be changed. Other major aspects of your life could also change, which are more challenging. For instance, you may have to change churches or your child's school. You may even have to move away from your extended family, good friends, and familiar community where you find security and comfort. Yes, a decision to take a new job can result in the need to make more decisions, some of which might seem quite unrelated to the original decision.

We know the tragedy of relationships torn apart and the ripple effects of prideful decisions from 1 Samuel 18:1–9. Saul was terribly prideful and unable to celebrate the victories of David. After successful battles, praises were sung in the streets. Saul was recognized for conquering thousands, but David was recognized for conquering tens of thousands. Saul's pride extinguished the close relationship he had with David and ultimately with his own son, Jonathan, who was David's best friend.

Before we can move ahead in our lives, we sometimes have to say, "I was wrong."

Before we can progress in our lives, there are occasions when we have to decide to say, "I was wrong." That can be difficult if we once proudly announced to the world that our original decision was absolutely "right." In such situations, it can be more comfortable to be quiet and hope for the best. Because of the *veil of pride,* many times we keep our mouths shut and stick with a bad decision regardless of how foolish that may be. In the case of the "dream job," you might have to admit to family, friends, and your business associates that it was not as "dreamy" as you initially thought! Just hoping for the best can result in disappointment. Inflexibility in the face of changed circumstances can bring trouble in your life. One bad decision can easily lead to many more, until one day you look back with sorrow at the dreams and opportunities you've missed and say, "If I had only known then what I know now, I would have done things a different way."

CHANGING OUR MIND CAN BE EVIDENCE OF COURAGE, NOT COWARDICE

We read in Mark 15:33–39 that the Roman centurion who helped crucify Jesus Christ realized as Jesus took his last breath that he truly was the Son of God. Imagine the opportunities this centurion missed to demonstrate courage at the very end. However, surely this changed perspective altered his future decisions.

As our perspectives change in this ever-changing, less-than-perfect world, we continually choose between firmly holding our ground or backing up to reconsider previous decisions. No one likes to "retreat," but here's the paradox: Admitting that our perspective has changed doesn't cause us to back up; many times it is the first step that allows us to move forward. Admitting that we are wrong doesn't inhibit our progress; it accelerates it.

Conversely, there are times when trying to move forward when we should alter our course causes us to lose ground. Failing to tear away the *veil of pride* can

> *Changing our mind can be evidence of courage, not cowardice.*

set us back. Reluctance to change our mind can also affect others who share our situation or circumstance. When we miss the opportunity to change our minds, to a certain extent, others will miss opportunities, too.

We should strive every day of our lives to modify our *veil of pride* because it blocks our view and hinders our progress.

THE MASTER PLAN

God's ultimate purpose will always prevail. God knows, allows, and understands that through human choice many paths and plans will be altered. Many times we travel down rabbit trails of sin and eventually find that we need to change our mind and travel in a different direction.

God had a master plan when he placed the Ark of the Covenant behind a veil. The Ark was a tangible example that symbolized the separation between a holy God and a sinful people. We know that Jesus Christ was the fulfillment of that plan. God tore that veil (Matt. 27:50–51) and opened the way to a direct relationship for all who believe.

From the Bible, we learn the significance of opening up to "big-picture" perspectives. If we only read the Old Testament, our perspective is limited because our knowledge would stop at the point where a veil separates us from God. But as we read further, our perspective changes because our knowledge increases. This example of the veil being torn changes our perspective. It is not just a small one—it's one of eternal significance. In fact, while we are on earth, we will never fully comprehend its magnitude, but we can understand why God did it from the New Testament.

Admitting that we are wrong doesn't inhibit our progress; it accelerates it.

As we read "the rest of the story" about God's master plan and experience it in life, we gain greater insight so we can influence others to rethink their positions as well. How would the people in Old Testament times have reacted if they had been able to read what the future held as written in the New Testament about the veil's purpose? Certainly, many

> *Jesus could have changed the course of history by saving himself.*

would have changed their perspective about the original veil if they had known what the future would offer beyond the torn veil.

Of course, some would have dug in their heels and said, "Once a veil, always a veil. That's the way it's always been, so that's the way it will always be...we have a veiled relationship with God." There is a sadness (rooted in pride) when people don't change their minds and miss the truth about God's plan to unite with us.

Even in New Testament times, some of the religious leaders did not realize the Scriptures they studied so diligently were fulfilled in the person of Jesus Christ. Because Jesus did not fit their preconceived notion of the Messiah—instead coming as a humble, suffering servant, not a conquering political figure—the people had the Son of God put to death rather than change their perspective. On the other hand, Jesus could have changed the course of history by saving himself. Many of the witnesses to the crucifixion called out for him to do just that so that he would prove to the skeptics that he was indeed the Son of God. But Jesus did not "flip flop" in an effort to save himself. Instead, he honored his Father and was used to fulfill the prophesies that caused him to lose his life on our behalf.

It's not a sign of weakness to change our minds when necessary, but like Jesus' decision to pay the ultimate price for our sins, we should also be brave enough to stick to our deeply held beliefs when they are used to love God and to love neighbor. It's an indication of healthy self-confidence when we learn how to discern between times when we need to change our mind and times when we should hold firmly to our deeply held beliefs.

Jesus did not "flip flop" in an effort to save himself.

Just like changing course every now and then can actually be very good, so is maintaining our fundamental convictions, if they are grounded in the truth. When our *veil of pride* is removed, we will make better decisions about our life's circumstances. When we get to that point, we will be empowered to navigate through ever-changing perspectives to ever-higher accomplishments!

Can you see past your *veil of pride* to envision a better future for yourself and for the ones that you love?

Take a good look at your veil of pride—God does!

Parting Your Veil

1. Have you ever "stuck to your guns" even though you were wrong? Why couldn't you change your position?

2. How hard is it to admit that you were wrong?

3. Does God change his mind?

4. Has the *veil of pride* kept you from changing your perspective on some matters of the past in which you should have yielded?

5. What might change in your life if you lowered your *veil of pride* a few notches?

4 ⦚ Seeking 20/20 Vision

Veil of Shortsightedness

Most of us are born with 20/20 vision; some are even blessed with better than 20/20. But as we get older, our vision deteriorates. Around age forty, it seems that most of us are reaching for a pair of "readers" from a case at the local drug store.

Even though we can live without our sense of sight, it is important and enhances our lives. We need our eyes for reading, driving a car, doing our work, seeing loved ones, and for differentiating the vibrant colors of God's creation.

Our eyes, like our fingerprints, are unique only to us.

We have hundreds of other things that we need and use our vision for every day.

Our eyes, like our fingerprints, are also unique to us. They differ in shape, color, size and other ways. Our eyes complement our individual identity.

Do you know if you exercise your eyes, you can broaden your peripheral vision? You can develop your ability to "see" life more honestly, joyfully, and reverently if you also exercise your unique perspective. A starting point to expanding your vision could be to intentionally pause every now and then to take a good look at the world around you.

LOOKING AROUND FOR THE BIGGER PICTURE

God put eyes in the front of our head and also created us to walk upright for a purpose. We are supposed to stay focused and to move forward in life. As a result, we naturally tend to view most of life from one perspective, which is horizontal. However, God does not want us to maintain tunnel vision. We don't spend as much time looking up, down, sideways or behind because we typically look straight ahead.

> *God does not want us to maintain tunnel vision.*

Think about it for a few minutes...how often do you intentionally pause to really look around you—to exercise the ability God has given you to view life from a wider viewpoint? When we make a habit of looking around, instead of only looking at life horizontally, we can experience more of life. "Looking around" actually sets the stage for dreaming, prompts us to ponder a "bigger picture," and prepares us to better utilize the opportunities that God offers us. When we commune more fully with God by taking in the fullness of God's creation, we will become more open to what God has in store for us and wants of us.

Next time you are outside, try this: take a few moments and look up at the birds of the air or at the tree tops. If it's nighttime, look up at the stars in the sky. Allow yourself to dream about what else may be up there; you may notice how your thoughts naturally turn to God. In Psalm 8:3–4, King David asked:

> *When I look at your heavens, the work of your fingers, the moon and the stars that you have established; what are human beings that you are mindful of them, mortals that you care for them?*

Does your vision allow you to see miracles today? Many people say miracles are of the past; yet this psalm describes the miracle of creation that continues each day. How about the birth of a baby—a miracle! The human body and all its intricacies that sustain life within each of us is another daily miracle. God set all this in motion in the very beginning, when he created everything.

Like David, shouldn't we all be more intentional about considering something bigger than us? Of course, God is not only in the sky, but is all around us, too. God is also in our hearts, minds, and souls.

Sometimes, pausing and seeking to align our visions with God's visions for our lives can enliven us and can help us break through our *veil of shortsightedness.* How does God help us "see" better? Very often, God's help comes to us through the assistance of other people when they offer us their points of view.

VISION CORRECTION—SEEKING HELP IS THE FIRST STEP

As your eyesight fades, we can correct it by wearing glasses. For centuries, people accepted eyeglasses as the only "fix" for both nearsighted and farsighted people. Then, only a few decades ago, contact lenses were invented, and vision correction took a giant step forward. But a few people continued to look around—dreaming about correcting sight *without* glasses or contacts. These people's dreams sparked ideas that eventually led to research and extremely careful testing.

From those tests, surgically corrective procedures were invented to permanently correct eyesight without glasses or contacts. Lasik is one such procedure that is commonly used today to restore people's sight to "near perfect," which is considered 20/20 vision. Basically, laser beams, guided by a doctor's steady hand, burn your eyeballs into submission! Well, it's really not as brutal and scary as it sounds...here's how it works.

Initially, you meet with the doctor to see if you are a "candidate" for the surgery, but don't count on an individual consultation. The surgery is so popular that there will probably be several other people in your orientation. Everyone in the room is full of questions: What's the procedure like? Does it hurt? Can I see immediately after it's over? Could this make me blind if something goes wrong? What are the possible side effects? What is the recovery time? Will I miss work? How

> *Another aspect of your vision that is even more unique is your perspective.*

much does it cost? Why do I have to sign a "hold harmless" form that indicates all of the bad things that could happen as a result of the surgery?

To most people, the benefits associated with near-perfect vision outweigh all of the items in question, so they consider the next step.

Accepting help—the next step

After each of the anticipated questions is answered and you listen to the doctor's summation, your fears begin to mount. You realize more than ever that you only have one pair of eyes. It hits you like a ton of bricks—if something goes wrong, you could possibly lose your eyesight! If the extreme of losing your eyesight were not a possibility, why do the papers you have to sign say that it is possible?

Anyway, in all of the debate with yourself, you realize that you have a big decision to make. You can either allow the fear of the unknown to keep you from moving forward with the surgery, or you can tame your fears and live an enriched life with much better vision after the corrective procedure. Are you going to *accept* all the risks involved to reap the reward of near-perfect eyesight, without glasses or contacts?

Often our veil of shortsightedness keeps us from seeing ourselves clearly.

Perhaps the bigger question is: Will you accept someone else's help so that you can see clearly again?

The last step—maintain faith

After you have been accepted as a candidate for surgery by the doctor and accept all the associated risks, you commit to the surgery. As your tension and stress increase to another level, you actually feel excited, too. With all of the paperwork signed, you are ready to go!

On the day of the procedure, your mind is racing and you begin to talk to the doctor; you need some reassurance:

"Doctor, my palms are sweaty this morning; are yours? You said that this will not hurt very much…right? That pill you gave me to settle my emotions before this procedure…how long does it take to work? Do you realize these are my only eyes you are about to laser?" As you lie on the procedure table, feet cold as ice, you understand why there is a prepayment policy. Your smart doctor instituted that policy for chickens like you. As you lie flat on your back, looking up you begin to pray that all goes well.

You continue to carry on a dialog with the doctor and you mentally prepare yourself for the looming surgery. Maybe you are sort of talking to God at the same time: *"I can't believe I am about to do this. My eyes are precious to me; they mean almost as much as life itself. Sure, I could live without them, but I would miss so much of life if I were blind. I know that my current sight is fuzzy and needs to be corrected, but at what physical cost? I don't want to lose the fuzzy sight that I do have. One more time, Doctor…are you OK doing this procedure? If you are OK, I guess I'm OK too; I think I am ready to do this. I trust you, Doc. Did I say my palms are sweaty… God, are you here—I can't see you, but I feel your presence; can you help me get through this? I think the pill is kicking in…I sure feel weird."*

You lie there on the procedure table, feet cold as ice…

In an instant, your dialog with yourself, the doctor, and God fades to black.

Before you know it, you wake up—Praise God— within a few minutes, modern medicine has corrected your blurred vision. You made the choice to accept the assistance of the doctor to help you see clearly again! As the effects of the sleeping pill wear off, it dawns on you that God was watching out for you while you were "under." God was with you all along. And you wonder if God is smiling as much as you are—you now have 20/20 vision again!

In our life journeys, we will encounter many opportunities as well as obstacles. We need to "see the possibilities" all around us to use God's provided resources. Seek assistance, accept help, and maintain faith to seize the possibilities. Is God smiling or wondering why you didn't trust in the first place?

God was watching out for you while you were "under."

There are many great scriptural examples of those who did not accept someone else's help, who relied on themselves and were very shortsighted. One of those people is Lot. As we read in Genesis 13:5–15, Lot was given a choice of land from his uncle, Abraham. Lot chose what appeared to be the best, the lushest land, having the best livestock and being the most valuable. Rather than discuss options with his uncle, who was offering a gift, Lot chose the land next to Sodom and Gomorrah, which was full of very sinful people.

Eventually, Lot had to flee for his life, and in the process lost his land, livestock and even his wife. If only Lot had used his peripheral vision, asked questions, sought counsel from one who was wiser and more experienced and a follower of God, his life might have been very different.

King Rehoboam also sought counsel from the wise elders, rejected it, and chose to follow the advice of his young peers instead. He used his power to make life miserable for the Israelites and continued the division between the northern and southern kingdoms (1 Kings 12:3–16).

SEEKING CORRECTION OF THE OTHER KIND OF VISION

Another aspect of your vision is even more unique—your perspective. Just as your eyes are unique to you, no one else sees life the way you do. One person can stand next to another person and look at the same scene (even without blinking), and each of them will see it with a different perspective. Just as eyesight can deteriorate with age, perspective can become compromised or distorted by life's changing circumstances. If we are close-minded to new ideas, our *veil of shortsightedness* can keep us from clearly seeing the world around us and can even separate us from acting upon the visions that God bestows upon us.

Does your vision (the type that has nothing to do with your eyesight) need to be corrected every so often? When it does, do you allow someone else (or God) to help you with the correction, or does your *veil of shortsightedness* sometimes get in the way? When your physical eyesight needs to be corrected, things get blurry, so you can easily recognize that you need to seek assistance. Whether you choose glasses, contacts, or surgery, you can correct your physical vision. But it's not as easy to get help when your perspective needs

> *He used his power to make life miserable for the Israelites.*

an occasional adjustment. Often our *veil of shortsightedness* keeps us from seeing ourselves clearly, so we don't recognize that we need help in the first place. Other people don't have to be experts—like your eye doctor—to help lift that veil; but they can help you restore proper perspective when it needs an occasional adjustment. That's how God intended the community of faith to work—people helping one another through life, using others to help us make necessary corrections.

Ultimately, God is the great physician and will help us see our lives clearly as things get out of focus. We have to ask for assistance and thereafter we must accept the responsibility to accept the assistance extended to us. God does not use laser beams to correct our vision nor will we be "burned into submission." But sometimes God will temper us as our perspectives are improved. Saul/Paul certainly was

> *God is the great physician and will help us see our lives clearly.*

tempered by God! Paul's vision needed to be corrected as did his perspective of the Christian faith. He was struck blind by God for three days. After that time, Paul accepted the help of others and devoured learning and living the Christian lifestyle. He became one of the greatest evangelists and church planters of all time (Acts 9:1–22)!

Maybe our experiences are not as dramatic as Paul's, but we sometimes have questions for God similar to the ones that we asked the Lasik doctor. *"Does it hurt to change my perspective, God? Will I be able to see my life better if my veil of shortsightedness is lifted? Are there any side effects to changing my perspective; I mean, are there negative effects when my life's vision is adjusted? What is the cost to my life and the lives of those around me if I maintain my veil of shortsightedness?"*

CINDY NEEDED AN ADJUSTMENT

God can assist us with all of our needs, if we will ask for help. To give help, God uses our prayers to dialog with us directly, and God also uses others.

Once you allow your vision to be corrected (whether your physical or nonphysical sight), you can begin to look around at your surroundings from a new and different perspective.

God uses our prayers to dialogue with us directly, and God also uses others.

The effect of shortsighted vision (and the beauty of gained peripheral vision) became extremely obvious to me during my very first seminary class: Basic Intro to the Bible. I grew up in the church and at this point in my career had been on staff at a local church for more than six years. Since I taught others about the Bible, I anticipated this class to be...let's politely say "elementary." Honestly, at that time in my life I felt I had a pretty good understanding of scripture so I really did not want to be in such a fundamental class with all of the other "beginners."

I will never forget when it hit me in that class how shortsighted I was. My blinders, which had confined me to a tunnel vision I did not even know I had, were removed in that class.

As the professor lectured and I took notes, things were revealed to me that I had never known. My tunnel vision perspective of the Bible was transformed into a wider, more peripheral vision. This was how I needed to see God's world, too—from a much broader perspective.

For me, the scriptures came alive in Basic Intro to the Bible!

I learned how to move beyond simply reading the Bible, trying to understand who's who, timelines, and facts, to searching the meaning behind the stories that had been inspired by God! I became intrigued with how God's Word applies to our lives today.

God is hunting for hearts—including yours.

After my "awakening," I prayed that I would never limit God's Word again by having such a narrow perspective that I failed to see the bigger picture. I still pray that prayer today; I now know that in those early years I had created a barrier between myself and God—it was my *veil of shortsightedness.*

I needed a vision adjustment during that time of my Christian walk. And I find that, as an extension of my humanity, I still need those adjustments regularly.

We all need vision adjustments along our life journeys. Fortunately, all we need to do to get an adjustment is to humbly seek (and then accept) an adjustment.

Oh, by the way, the answer is "no" . . . whether it's your eyesight or your perspective, it doesn't hurt to get your vision corrected every so often. It just takes a little courage on your part to seek out the needed assistance from others and from God. We begin to see the world from a wider and more peripheral perspective when we allow our faith to overcome the veils that keep us from seeing life clearly.

WHAT TO LOOK FOR

We look for so many things throughout life. Having clear and peripheral vision is important. Consider the spies Joshua sent into Jericho (an enemy territory, but one destined to be claimed for God) ahead of the Israelites. Surely the spies had to be very observant of all their surroundings as they entered Jericho. They also had been willing to accept the assistance of Rahab to hide them for their protection. Rahab and the spies gave witness to their faith that God was with them (Joshua 2:1–27; 6:22–25).

And how about Zaccheus (Luke 19:1–9)? Zaccheus was a rich tax collector who wanted desperately to see the man called Jesus. The crowds had gathered and he could not see; but he was NOT shortsighted. He positioned himself high in the syca-

> *It doesn't hurt to get your vision corrected every so often. It just takes a little courage.*

more tree to see. His seeing led to believing, which led to hospitably inviting Jesus Christ to his home. The people were very shortsighted, as evidenced in verse 7.

GOD IS HUNTING FOR HEARTS

If we go on a scavenger hunt outside or looking for specific species of plant life, maybe hunting deer or turkeys, whatever...our natural instinct is to look around, side to side, and down at the ground for evidence of that for which we are looking. We may look up for nests in trees or to see what the weather is doing as part of our hunt. Women go to the mall and hunt for bargains. Children continually hunt for fun. Older folks hunt for people who will listen to their stories. Single people hunt for mates. Teenagers hunt for excitement and friends. Many people hunt on the Internet for information.

What veils in your life cloud your vision and hamper your unique perspective?

Since humans were created in God's own image, isn't it interesting to consider that God must also have hunter's eyes? God is hunting for hearts—yours included. Is your *veil of shortsightedness* keeping you from seeing that God is hunting for you, wanting you to give your heart to him first and others thereafter?

What are some things in life for which you are hunting? As you continuously look for things you need or for things you want, you are always in God's sight. God has 100 percent peripheral vision, which means that God is everywhere at once—he is omnipresent. God is also omniscient—all seeing, all knowing. Of course we are not God. We don't have 100% omniscient vision. But we do have peripheral vision, and we should intentionally use it.

Using our peripheral vision will allow us to lower our *veil of shortsightedness* so that we can live more fulfilled lives. With corrected vision, we naturally become more open to changing our minds on some of our past decisions, biases, stereotypes, etc., as well as also changing our perspectives as we move ahead. We will also discover the vastness of God's world and how much there is to learn, live, and enjoy.

So where are the veils in your life that cloud your vision and hamper your unique perspective? Are you resistant to letting others help you? What help do you need to accept so that your life is more fulfilled? The bigger question is: Are you resistant to letting God assist you with all of your needs, wants, and desires? Are you trying to veil yourself from God's watchful eye, even though that is impossible?

> *Do you resist letting God assist you with all of your needs, wants and desires?*

Moving forward, will you more readily accept guidance from a trusted friend, a professional, and God to help you see more clearly as you walk along your life journey? Paul teaches in 2 Corinthians that we are to walk by faith—faith that God walks with us and has given us every resource needed to live a more fulfilled life.

Are you ready to expand and enhance your vision to gain a greater perspective on your life . . . or will you remain shortsighted, resistant to the assistance that the great physician wants to give?

Take a good look at your veil of shortsightedness—God does!

Parting Your Veil

1. Have you ever made a shortsighted decision that you later regretted? What was the result of your shortsightedness?

2. What specific actions could you take in your life that would allow God to correct any shortsightedness in your vision?

3. How can the community of faith help you improve your perspective?

4. In what ways can the *veil of shortsightedness* keep us from trusting God more perfectly?

5. What might change in your life if you could see beyond your *veil of shortsightedness?*

5 ‖ Forging Partnerships

Veil of Self-Reliance

L ike pieces that fit neatly into a jigsaw puzzle or gloves that slip perfectly over our hands, so it is with partners who fit nicely into our lives.

Have you ever experienced the joy of a meaningful partnership? Are you blessed with any partnerships now? Can you close your eyes and visualize the faces of people whom you could call partners? Because we are made in God's own image, do you see God's face somewhere within this vision?

THE DESIRE FOR PARTNERSHIPS

When you were a child, did you ever ask another kid to be your blood brother or sister? Did you have a secret handshake with a trusted friend, such as the pinky-to-pinky handshake? These innocent acts of youth signified a partnership that was meaningful to both you and your friend.

As we grow older, our desire for partnerships remains strong…a spouse, business partners, community partners, church partners, and so forth. We enter other types of "partnerships" too—in college did you join a sorority or fraternity and pledge to be loyal to others for life? While serving in the military, were you so committed to others that you vowed to lay down your life for them? As a Christian, are your commitments to your brothers and sisters in Christ at least as strong as your commitments to your blood relatives? What about your accountability partners?

Have you ever had a partnership that was so strong that you looked your partner in the eye and promised never to forsake him or her, no matter what?

"I want to be your partner." These six words, when spoken to another person, have the power to transform relationships! When two people agree to be partners, something very special occurs. In an instant, *my* dreams become *our* dreams; *my* opportunities become *our* opportunities; *my* perspectives become *our* perspectives; and *my* inquisitive spirit becomes *our shared* inquisitive spirits.

Since God doesn't make mistakes, our differences must have a purpose.

But with all this talk about partners and partnerships, what is a partnership, really? The dictionary definition says that a partnership is "the voluntary association of two or more people for the purpose of establishing and engaging in a mutual interest or desire." Unfortunately, that definition doesn't mention three primary ingredients that transform everyday relationships into partnerships: sharing, complementing, and trust.

SHARING LIFE WITH OTHERS

God created each of us with unique talents and temperaments. Since God doesn't make mistakes, our differences must have a purpose. Could it be that God wants us to *complement* each other?

To *complement* doesn't mean to praise or flatter. That word is *compliment.* We compliment people when they have a nice appearance or act in a particularly praiseworthy manner. The word *complement* has to do with *completing.* When we share our unique talents and gifts with others, we make up for what they lack and vice versa. We *complement* them by making them more whole. That's the way that God designed us—to complement one another. We do that by mutually sharing ourselves with others. Sharing is freely giving of our time, talents, and treasure to others. It's also about receiving, with grace, what others desire to share with us.

> *When we share with others, we make up for what they lack and vice versa.*

Openly sharing our lives with others requires a key element that is sometimes hard to allow, which is to let others temper us. Proverbs 27:17 tells us, *"Iron sharpens iron, and one person sharpens the wits of another."* Without others to challenge, encourage, and comfort us, we can become as useless as a dull knife.

Are you the type of person who prefers to fly through life solo, not really enjoying that tempering process that comes when others "complement" you? Do you like to do things alone most of the time? Do your actions suggest that you want to stay disconnected from people, neither wanting to share with them nor allowing them to share with you? Do you behave as though you wear an invisible sign that says *"No Partners Allowed"* by looking down when you

> *Do you behave as though you wear a sign that says "No Partners Allowed"?*

walk by other people or looking away when someone is talking to you?

If so, your heart, which might be hindered by the *veil of self-reliance,* may need to be softened. God can give you the desire and confidence to share your life with others, if you ask for that in your prayers. If you will allow this to happen, you can be sure that you will be "sharpened" when you invite others into your life!

Partners are different, on purpose!

Partnerships that enhance our lives come in many forms and can serve many different purposes. If you are married, your primary and most important human partnership is supposed to be with your spouse. Proceeding outward, you should also have differing types of partnerships with your children, parents, and other relatives.

Beyond your family circle, it is also healthy to forge key partnerships with friends, business associates, and people in other areas of your life. The appropriate "order" of our partnership choices is certainly important, but what "type" of partner are we supposed to seek?

Fortunately, the Bible gives us some insight into what type of persons we, as Christians, should partner with. In 2 Corinthians 6:14–15, the apostle Paul gives us great advice:

Do not be mismatched with unbelievers. For what part-
nership is there between righteousness and lawlessness? Or
what fellowship is there between light and darkness? What
agreement does Christ have with Beliar? Or what does a
believer share with an unbeliever?

So as Christians, some of our most important partnerships will be within the church, with fellow believers. In
fact, these relationships are to be so supportive, unified,
and transparent that the Bible describes believers as members of one body, the body of Christ. However, even as
one body, the parts have different purposes and each part
contributes to the whole.

In Romans 12:4–8, we see how the whole body is supposed to relate to its parts:

For as in one body we have many members, and not all the
members have the same function, so we, who are many,
are one body in Christ, and individually we are members
one of another. We have gifts that differ according to the
grace given to us: prophecy, in proportion to faith; minis-
try, in ministering; the teacher, in teaching; the exhorter,
in exhortation; the giver, in generosity; the leader, in dili-
gence; the compassionate, in cheerfulness.

Our differences are actually gifts that God gives us
that allow us to complement one another so that the entire
body functions better. Each of our relational partnerships
can offer a variety of benefits in terms of love, encour-
agement, accountability, support, knowledge, guidance,

joy, laughter, business knowledge, and more. But none of our worldly partners (not even our spouse) can be totally complementary.

WE NEED MORE THAN JUST OTHER PEOPLE

Even though God places people in our lives to complement us, there is only one partner who can totally complete us. Only God is sufficient for our every need; God is the ultimate partner! But even though God is all we need to be fulfilled, God still desires for us to have even more.

That "more" is our outward and mutual relationship with God's other children. And God's primary plan includes a foundational element that we are all supposed to understand before we form our partnerships in life. God wants us to love him, love others, and love ourselves too.

Only God is sufficient for our every need; God is the ultimate partner!

The relationship that God desires for us is beautifully stated in 1 John 4:7–21.

As is usually the case, we are also supposed to mirror God's example in our relationships with others:

> *Beloved, let us love one another, because love is from God; everyone who loves is born of God and knows God. Whoever does not love does not know God, for God is love. God's love was revealed among us in this way: God sent his only Son into the world so that we might live through him. In this is love, not that we loved God but that he loved us and sent his Son to be the atoning sacrifice for our sins. Beloved, since God loved us so much, we also ought*

to love one another. No one has ever seen God; if we love one another, God lives in us, and his love is perfected in us.

By this we know that we abide in him and he in us, because he has given us of his spirit. And we have seen and do testify that the Father has sent his Son as the Savior of the world. God abides in those who confess that Jesus is the Son of God and they abide in God. So we have known and believe the love that God has for us.

> **God intentionally gives different gifts to us for the purpose of mutual sharing.**

God is love, and those who abide in love abide in God, and God abides in them. Love has been perfected among us in this: that we may have boldness on the day of judgment, because as he is, so are we in this world. There is no fear in love, but perfect love casts out fear; for fear has to do with punishment, and whoever fears has not reached perfection in love. We love because he first loved us. Those who say "I love God" and hate their brothers or sisters, are liars; for those who do not love a brother or a sister whom they have seen, cannot love God whom they have not seen. The commandment we have from him is this: those who love God must love their brothers and sisters also.

COMPLEMENTARY TRAITS WE SHARE

When we fail to form partnerships with others, we are less complete than if we would have accepted this primary gift that God wants to give us—the greatest gift of all, to love and be loved! God intentionally gives different gifts to different people for the purpose of mutual sharing, but we are to love one another while we are sharing life with each other. We are to celebrate our differences, also in love.

We have so much to gain from people who are unlike us. Conversely, we also have much to give in return. But when choosing partners, we seem to instinctively gravitate toward people who are like us in most ways. That's not wrong; it's just human nature. Even Jesus chose to spend more time with certain disciples than others. That wasn't wrong either, nor was it "human nature" when Jesus did it; instead he chose to spend more time with some and less time with others. We are allowed to choose our partners and they choose us.

> *When we choose partners, we seem to gravitate toward people like us.*

Whether in a church, business, family setting or other area where there are partnership opportunities, it makes sense to initially look for others who share similar passions, perspectives, dreams, and even our sense of humor. However, an unexpected thing often happens as our relationships deepen with seemingly like-minded people. The people who we thought were almost "just like us" turn out to be very different—but that's really a blessing too. Yes, God created each of us to be uniquely different on purpose!

Regardless of differences, good partners need to be patient and sensitive to each other's needs and desires, just like God is with us. Sometimes one partner moves at lightning speed while the other crawls at a snail's pace. So it also is with our relationship with God…have you ever moved at "your" schedule, instead of following God's timeline? How does it work out when we try to run ahead of others, exceeding a pace that is supposed to be shared? These differences in timing may not be wrong on either side, but nonetheless can cause one or both partners frustration.

Do you wonder if God gets frustrated with us when we run off on our own, leaving our Lord and Savior out of our lives? Partners must be considerate of each other as they travel through life side by side—regardless of who your partner is, especially God!

God walks with us at all times, no matter what and even if we venture off on our own agenda. We should strive to do the same with our partners. During times of trial, one partner may need to carry the other or simply offer standby support as needed. The bonds of a partnership are continuously being tempered in the furnaces of a shared life; it's in difficult times that partners can grow closer. Life's victories and defeats can also strengthen partnerships. Whether the shared circumstances are good or they are difficult, partnerships grow stronger as experiences are shared.

It's just like God's unconditional love—whether in hard times or times of plenty, God always stands by us, no matter what.

TRUSTED PARTNERSHIPS

Contrary to some secular beliefs, our first and most trusted partner is not supposed to be our spouse, nor our family or friends. It is to be God. As Christians, God should be at the center of all of our relationships and completely trusted.

Our partnerships with other people should closely resemble, but not completely mirror, our relationship and partnership with God. Why should we differentiate in the levels of trust we allow? Well, because there's one significant difference between us and God—God is perfect, and we are not.

Neither your spouse, family members, friends nor anyone else is perfect. For this reason, our partnerships with other people will (from time to time) invariably fall short of our expectations, as well as the expectations of our partner. In fact, even our partnership with God is only half perfect, because one-half depends on us. But because in this life we are "moving on to perfection," God will always be with us, every step of the way—even if we ignore God by running wild every now and then!

Despite our imperfections, God chose to enter into (and maintain) an intimate partnership with us. In fact, the Bible says that we are God's workmanship, created to do good works, which God prepared in advance for us to do (Eph. 2:10). In other words, God desires to work in and through us for eternal purposes. How's that for an amazing partnership!

We did not initiate our partnership with God. God chose us before the creation of the world. We were known by God even before we were born (Psalm 139:13–16). Therefore, we can be secure in the knowledge that God will never leave us or forsake us, as our imperfect human partners might do. People break commitments, but God never does that, even when our affections are fickle. God never waivers from the intimate relationship that he desires to share with us. God promises that our partnership with him will last for the rest of our worldly lives…and also for eternity as we spend it in heaven! Isn't it awesome that as Christians, God is on our side?

Could you think of God as your most trusted partner in life, if you stopped and really thought about your relationship in a different way?

Reciprocally responsive

Even though God desires to be in the most intimate and primary partnership with you, unlike any other type of partnerships you have with other people, you must willingly respond in order to participate. God will not force you to reciprocate the invitation to "partner" with him, but will patiently wait for you to respond, on your own timeline.

Have you ever sensed God nudging you to form an important partnership of some type?

Maybe you didn't hear an audible voice say, "I want to be your partner in this endeavor," and perhaps you did not feel or see a "sign" of some type, but for some reason you felt inclined to take a step in response to God's call. Did you simply ignore that nudging, or did you accept the partnership invitation?

> *God will not force you to reciprocate the invitation to "partner" with him.*

Those types of invitations often come in the form of opportunities to reach out to others at home, at church, at work, and in the community. Thinking back, do you remember how you responded when you received those invitations or that nudging from God? If you accepted them, can you now see the good results from your obedience to God's subtle call?

On the other hand, if you ignored invitations to be a partner with God in some sort of worldly endeavor (and with others who wanted to partner with you), why did you

How can we lower the veil of self-reliance that distances us from others?

do that? What (or who) kept you from simply saying, "Yes, Lord, I will do that with you"?

Or if you are really honest with yourself, have you become so "self-reliant" that you just don't want to do anything with or for anyone else, even with God?

THE *VEIL OF SELF-RELIANCE*

The authenticity of our partnerships is directly proportional to the level of trust and faith that we have with other people, and with God. Because complete trust and faith is such a rare and fragile commodity—due to the flawed nature of human beings—it's easy for the *veil of self-reliance* to be drawn over our spiritual eyes. We should resist Satan's temptation to abandon trust and faith by trusting more and having even more faith! We do this when we complement others, by sharing ourselves with them.

How can we lower the *veil of self-reliance* that distances us from others? We can do it by first properly ordering strong partnerships—God first, our spouse second, family third, and then others. Thereafter, we intentionally have more faith and trust in our partners. Those are overlooked fringe benefits that come from trusted partnerships.

Meaningful partnerships help us better resist the temptation to be skeptical of (or mistrustful of) others. Skepticism and mistrust can cause us to be more self-reliant, thus raising and maintaining a veil between ourselves and the others with whom we might partner.

Since Satan is in the business of dividing and conquering, he delights in his work when we become so self-reliant that we separate ourselves from others. We move away from the partnerships that God desires for our lives when we fall into Satan's trap!

Think about it this way—when our *veil of self-reliance* separates us from others and prevents us from forging the partnerships that we desire and need, we actually hold ourselves back from the way that God intends for his children to love one another.

WARNING—WARNING—WARNING!

But when we enter into partnerships with other people, some caution is advisable. Only God is 100 percent trustworthy. For this reason, it's actually unwise to completely trust others in the exact same capacity as we trust God. However, we are still supposed to love other people, even though they

Are you allowing your veil of self-reliance to isolate you from others?

are imperfect and they sometimes violate our trust. We are called to share with others and to allow God to fill in the gaps of their imperfections.

Let us not be so afraid of hurt and disappointment that we fail to love others enough to make ourselves vulnerable to them. Let's not allow the *veil of self-reliance* to keep us from forging meaningful partnerships with other people after we have formed our primary partnership with God.

A HEALTHY DOSE OF SELF EXAMINATION

- Are you allowing your *veil of self-reliance* to isolate you from others?
- To whom have you fully entrusted yourself in the past? How did that work out?
- Have you ever tried to partner with someone you did not fully trust?
- How do you normally pick your partners, or do they usually select you?
- Is God *really* your most trusted partner in your mind and heart?

God desires to be at the center of all of our relationships and partnerships. Just as Jesus called his first disciples by saying, *"Come, follow me"* (Matt. 4:19, Mark 2:14),

If we allow an unveiled partnership with God, we will learn to fully trust.

he invites us to partner with him in the work of the Kingdom of God. If we will allow a completely unveiled partnership with God, we will learn how to *fully* trust. We then can do a better job of entering into and maintaining more unveiled partnerships with others. Isn't it amazing that the omnipotent, omniscient, omnipresent God who created the universe desires to be in a completely trusted covenant partnership with us?

It's amazing that God created human beings with so many differences on purpose, so that we can complement one another in life. As you pray today that your *veil of self-reliance* be lifted, will you also reflect on what it means to be the best partner you can be? Yes, those six simple words, *"I want to be your partner"* have the power to transform your life, especially when Jesus Christ is the one who is hearing you say that.

Take a good look at your veil of self-reliance—God does!

Parting Your Veil

1. Who was your best friend when you were a child? Did you feel that you had a special partnership with him or her? Do you still know that person well?

2. The authors suggest that the foundation of all relationships is love in Christ; after that, there is an order of who would be your most trusted partners. What does this mean to you?

3. Do you consider God to be your partner in life? Why or why not?

4. Do you feel that the *veil of self-reliance* has kept you from moving ahead with a business, a relationship, or even serving in the church?

5. What do you think might happen in your life if you lowered your *veil of self-reliance* just a little and started to trust other people more?

6 ‖ Seeking Appropriate Standards

Veil of Obsession

We all have certain personal standards that we've either been taught or learned on our own. Whether our standards are "high" or "low," as we attempt to compare them to other people's standards, we all have them and they are unique to us. We maintain standards of living, academic standards, moral standards, physical standards, ethical standards, professional standards, Christian standards, etc. Like our built-in veils, no two people in the world have the exact same type and/or level of standards—they differ from person to person.

What is an "appropriate standard"?

Why are standards often prefaced with an adjective such as "high," "low," or "minimum"? For instance, we regularly hear phrases like "low standard of living" or "the highest academic standard." We hear that a "minimum standard" was set, but what is a minimum standard?

Since God created all humans as equals, who's in a position to impose standards upon or to judge others? In the gospel of John, Jesus was being addressed by the Pharisees about giving a testimony and about being judged. In John 8:15–16, Jesus said to the Pharisees:

> *"You judge by human standards; I judge no one. Yet even if I do judge, my judgment is valid; for it is not I alone who judge, but I and the Father who sent me."*

What is an "appropriate standard" and who is qualified to judge what an appropriate standard is?

THE FOOL'S OPINION

Don't be alarmed before you read any further into this chapter; we're not going to suggest that all standards within our society should be completely relative or parallel or that certain standards should be measured and others should not. We simply observe that in matters of opinion, when other people are involved, we shouldn't too strongly insist that "our way" is the best (or only) way.

> *Who is qualified to judge what an appropriate standard is?*

Sometimes we can become blinded to other people's ideas because we don't understand their perspectives or because we desire so badly to impose our opinions and standards upon them. Proverbs 18:2 tells us: *"A fool takes no pleasure in understanding, but only in expressing personal opinion."*

When we hold too tightly to our own strong opinions and don't try to understand another person's point of view, it's easy for us to cross the line from being honest, accurate, and helpful to being obstinate, irritating, offensive, or even foolish. Opinions too rigidly espoused can separate us from other people, especially when we go too far and become obsessive.

Do you express your opinions so strongly that they affect your relationships?

Obsessed, possessive, and territorial

The word "obsessed" is a very strong descriptor. Most of us would balk if we were labeled with that word. We can become obsessive about our standards, but let's first look at what leads us to be that way.

> We shouldn't too strongly insist that "our way" is the best (or only) way.

As we explore the subject of our standards, let's consider a less intrusive word like "possessive." Who wouldn't admit to being possessive to some degree or another about certain things: time, family, job, rights, money, church, and so forth? After all, isn't it logical to think that if we are supposed to take care of the possessions that God entrusts us with, then aren't we supposed to be possessive to some degree or another? However, we can go too far and become extremely possessive or opinionated about certain things, can't we?

If we are honest with ourselves, we would also acknowledge that we can be "territorial" to some degree as well. We all have the human tendency to protect or defend what is important to us.

Because we don't like people infringing upon our privacy or trying to move into our territory, we resent it when other people start meddling in our personal business. For instance, we don't like it when people at work start encroaching on job responsibilities. We don't like people telling us what to do with our money or how to raise our children. We don't take it very well when politicians tamper with our rights. When these kinds of things happen, even mild-mannered people can become territorial. We like to protect our territories!

If people become very "territorial" and "possessive" they may become "obsessive." How about you? Have you set the bar so high in some area of your life that others find it difficult to meet your expectations? Do other people do things that drive you so crazy that you, in turn, make others miserable by imposing a *veil of obsession* upon them? What "standards" should you modify so that your obsessive tendencies are tempered, thus making the other people around you happier?

> *Opinions too rigidly espoused can separate us from other people.*

Do your standards affect your relationships by creating barriers or do they enhance them by providing much needed and appropriate structure? Have you considered modifying your inappropriate standards instead of imposing them upon others...or are you still expecting the others around you to conform to "your way"?

MODIFYING STANDARDS—NOT THE SAME AS LOWERING THEM!

Seeking to "modify" your standards to reach a level of mutual acceptance with someone else (or to satisfy yourself) is not in the same category as "lowering" your standards.

There's a monumental difference between lowering standards and modifying standards—here's why: When we lower a standard by which we have chosen to live, our integrity might be questioned, both personally and in the eyes of other people.

However, when we modify our standards, we are viewed as a person who is willing to adapt and be flexible when needed to make a situation better. We are open to the valuable ideas that other people might offer us. Paul tells us in Romans 12:2 to not be conformed to this world but be transformed by the renewing of our minds. He goes on to emphasize that we need each other because we have a variety of gifts (Romans 12:2–8).

Do you know people who believe that their standards are the most appropriate of all, no matter what changing circumstances are presented? Are you possibly one of those people? Who has the ability (or the right) to deem themselves as wise enough to expect that others always follow their lead or always abide by their established standards?

When we are both "territorial" and "possessive" we can become "obsessive."

In 1 Corinthians 3:18–20, Paul clears up this looming question very quickly...from God's perspective. He was speaking to the people of Corinth about how badly they missed the mark even though they regarded themselves as so smart. He writes:

Do not deceive yourselves. If you think you are wise in this age, you should become fools so that you may become wise.

For the wisdom of this world is foolishness with God. For it is written, "He catches the wise in their craftiness," and again, "The Lord knows the thoughts of the wise, that they are futile."

Instead of attempting to appear wise by setting worldly standards and then imposing them on others, shouldn't we seek the most appropriate standards— God's standards? Sure, it's hard to measure up to God's standards; in fact, it is impossible to measure up to all of God's standards. That's the reason we continuously fall short of God's standards and then try to modify them by intentionally setting standards "our way" instead of "God's way."

> *Modifying standards is not the same as lowering them!*

What is "God's way" as related to setting standards? What does it mean to be wise without becoming a fool in the process? To understand this better, let's examine two "worldly situations" where protection of territory added to a possessive nature yielded an "obsession."

The "dish war"—A scenario that may hit home

Here's a hypothetical situation with which you might be able to identify. This little sketch demonstrates how something that is really insignificant in the grand scheme of things can quickly escalate as two people's "humanistic standards" differ.

After a hard day at work, a married couple finishes an enjoyable dinner at home. Humming a favorite song to herself, the wife starts putting the dishes away. As she is closing the dishwasher door, the husband appears behind her and speaks. Here is how the discussion goes:

Husband: *"You loaded the dishwasher wrong again."*

Wife: *"What difference does it make how the dishes are arranged?"*

Husband: *"If you would have done it the way I showed you, you'd get more dishes in."*

Wife: *"Is it really that important to maximize space to the degree that you feel is right?"*

Husband: *"Well, it seems to me that it makes a big difference."*

Wife: *"Whatever…"*

The key phrase in this exchange is, *"Well, it seems to me,"* and the key word within that key phrase is *"me."* That phrase is worded to protect an imposed standard of how the husband thought that the dishes should be loaded. The key word *"me"* suggests that the standard is a personal one.

Now, let's look at the situation from both sides. The wife asked a good question when she said *"Is it really that important?"* She probably wonders why her husband considers this issue so crucial that he is willing to cause a rift over it, messing up a nice evening. She thinks to herself that it could be a matter of principle or pride to him. What could be causing this mild case of obsession about how the dishes are loaded? Is this really about the dishwasher?

Looking at the husband's position, he may feel that if he compromises, he will be lowering his established standards or even yielding to his wife's opinion that differs from his. Maybe she is wrong about how the dishes are loaded—he wonders how the dishwasher manual says to do it.

What is "God's way" as related to setting standards?

If his wife decided to yield to loading "his" way, would her standards then be modified or lowered? If the husband decided to yield by not saying anything about her method of loading, would the dishes still be adequately washed?

"WHATEVER" IS NOT AN ENDING

The wife and the husband both had decisions to make in the brief exchange, didn't they? They could have continued to challenge the dish loading procedures by pulling out the manual, or let the whole thing go. They could have compromised by keeping quiet. But in this scenario, in order to avoid further argument, she gave in and said, *"Whatever."*

But what she was really saying in code was: *"OK, Mr. Dish-Master, do it your way."* In turn, to avoid a further argument, the husband accepted that artificial olive branch of peace with a smirk. In fact, the husband and wife may have just agreed (without saying another word) that he should do the dishes from that point forward to avoid future conflicts.

But underneath this uneasy surface truce resentments might persist. Someday, perhaps when the husband comes home after a long trip and finds the sink full of dishes, tempers will boil over and a "mother of all dish wars" will ensue.

Both spouses had thought they were giving in or maybe even compromising, but really this skirmish was just setting the stage for a war that would eventually become bigger than just a pile of dishes!

Maybe you and your spouse or roommate don't fight over dishes, but chances are you have a few battlegrounds of your own where the *veil of obsession* could be lowered so that you can at least live more harmoniously.

ANOTHER HYPOTHETICAL SITUATION—KIDS ARE AFFECTED TOO!

Have you ever known parents who dictate to their children (and then broadcast to the world) something like this: "In our family, only straight As are acceptable in school"?

Parents have to be especially sensitive to the standards they set.

Who is qualified to set that sort of standard anyway? Parents are supposed to care for their children and to steer them in the right direction to be successful; however, how far is too far?

Parents have to be especially sensitive to the standards they set and the examples they demonstrate for their kids. Children learn the ways of the world from watching what their parents do and say.

Picture this: A parent and child sit down to discuss the start of a new school semester. Their verbal exchange goes like this:

Parent: *"You and everyone else know that in our family, we accept only As."*

Child: *"But other kids' parents say that Bs are ok too."*

Parent: *"Well, if other kids' parents said it is ok to jump off a cliff, would that make it ok for you to jump off of a cliff, too?"*

Child: *"What does jumping off a cliff have to do with my grades?"*

Parent: *"When you grow up, you will understand it."*

Child: *"I am really confused now."*

Parent: *"Well, it seems to me that I am the parent here and know what is best for you. When you move out you can set your own standards, but when you are under my roof, you will measure up to the standards I set."*

Child: *"Whatever…"*

Was this exchange about grades or about a parent's obsession with imposing and controlling the standards he or she has placed upon the child? If the child makes a "B," what might happen to the parent's pride, given that the broadcast to the world was "we only make As in our family"?

Are straight As a realistic standard to set for all children, no matter what their gifts and graces are? What if one child is a math or history whiz and another is more interested in music or art? Should both children be expected to make As in *all* of their courses? If an A is expected in all classes and a B is earned in one class, does that mean that the B is a perceived failure in a family that "only accepts As"?

Could it be that the "standard setter" actually failed to be a good parent to his or her child by trying to impose a perceived "normal" standard upon the child?

Society's "normal" standards

What impact does society have on our behavioral patterns that in turn influence our lives and our standards? We might recall some familiar "situational" TV shows to see what society considers as "normal" relationships.

Some shows—such as *Andy Griffith, Leave It to Beaver, Father Knows Best,* and *The Cosby Show*—present one picture of "normal," but they also clearly demonstrate that standards do differ from one family to the next.

Roseanne and *The Simpsons* paint quite a different picture of family life. Actually, there's no such thing as a "normal" family because who can judge between what is normal and what's not normal? Certain standards generically fit some situations while others are developed specifically to accommodate each family.

We also know that all families are different from each other. Even if one family did appear to be "normal," we can be sure it would be far from perfect!

Fred and Wilma

The Flintstones fell somewhere between society's perceived "normal" family dynamic and the slightly dysfunctional family system. Fred and Wilma Flintstone, for example, fought all the time due to their differences of opinion; they probably fought over dishes too. Remember how Fred yelled *"W-I-L-M-A!"* at the top of his lungs on every show? Was he stressed out from a bad day at the rock quarry, or was he merely trying to demonstrate his dominance as the "man of the house"?

Wilma Flintstone seemed to be the ideal housewife. She not only did the dishes but also cooked the meals, cleaned the house, took care of their daughter Pebbles, and catered to Fred's needs and wants. Fred expected Wilma to take care of him, and she usually did just that. She also seemed to have enough time to always wear full make up with freshly coiffed hair, even while working around the house. But she wasn't as subservient as she appeared. She knew exactly how to handle Fred—which "Fred-buttons" to push (or not to push), depending upon the situation.

> *The Flintstones lived a life that was far from perfect, but to them it was "normal."*

While pretending to always submit to Fred and the life they shared, she was actually always in control of the household and her husband. When Fred let off steam by roaring *"W-I-L-M-A,"* she kept a stiff upper lip.

Day after day, the Flintstones lived a life that was far from perfect, but to them, it was "normal."

Most of the time, neither person was wrong when they fussed and fought. Actually, it could be more accurate to say that there were times when they were both wrong, as they navigated through a life of cohabitation.

Fred and Wilma acted more like roommates than they did husband and wife, but in reality they were married, just like the Beaver's parents were. Fred and Wilma had just as much right to claim a "normal" marriage as the Cosbys did. The Flintstone family was different—but so were all the others—so *are* all the others. Your family is different too, but guess what—it is also "normal" as compared to some standard, somewhere!

And so it is with us…the dishwashers of our lives somehow get loaded, one way or another. We go back and forth to work and take occasional vacations. Our smiles turn to frowns every so often and then change back to smiles again, but our *veil of obsession* can remain wrapped around those that we care about the most…or at least, we maintain that veil with the ones with whom we live, work, and play.

How "obsessive"…are you?

How would your life change if you modified your standards to closely match the standards of those individuals who share their lives with you? More specifically, what if

What if you asked God to help you temper your veil of obsession?

you asked God to help you temper your *veil of obsession* so that you could live more harmoniously with your spouse, children, friends, coworkers, and so forth?

You may not be obsessive to the point of making others miserable, but would some areas in your life be more satisfying and productive if you'd simply make the effort to modify your standards?

If you think about it, do you see any areas where you are overly possessive or territorial? What standards should you modify to reach a more appropriate level? Remember, we're only suggesting that you consider modifying some of your standards, not lowering any of them!

Next time you are convinced that you're absolutely "right" about some standard you have imposed that others are balking at, pause and ask yourself if there could be a *veil of obsession* that you could lower a notch or two, without lowering your integrity at the same time.

> *Are you are overly possessive or territorial in any areas?*

After all, are you more interested in having the reputation of being "right in every situation" or of being "understanding when you need to be"? Are you more committed to your self-imposed standards or to your desire to share more fulfilled relationships?

Many times—perhaps most times—many of our veils can only be removed when one side moves first, without expecting any movement from the other side. Actually, healthy relationships only have one side! Two people on the same side have double the power; unity is good and divisiveness is not good. Add God to the mix of two people on the same side, and things can turn in an instant from good to excellent, or in situations of strain, things can progress from bad to at least good!

Lowering your *veil of obsession* by being willing to change your attitude from "my way" to "our way" is pleasing to God. However, modifying your attitude to endorse "God's way" rather than "your way" is much *more* pleasing to God.

So, what is "God's way" as related to standards?

THE GAMES WE PLAY WITH GOD

God gave us standards and he has been asking that we abide by those standards since the beginning of time. In the Garden of Eden, God set a standard—just one. He asked Adam and Eve not to eat the fruit from a certain tree. They ate the fruit any way and our sinful nature was unveiled.

God issued two new standards: Love God and love your neighbor.

After the "fruit incident," God modified that seemingly "simple standard."

In the Old Testament God gave us the original "top 10" list. The Ten Commandments were straightforward and they were not to be modified (Exodus 20:1–17). They were even etched into two stone tablets so that they could not be erased or changed. The Ten Commandments were clearly stated—the meaning behind each commandment is crystal clear. There is no gray area in any of the commandments.

But falling into the same pattern that Adam and Eve did, the people did not obey the Ten Commandments in Old Testament times and we still fall short of them today.

Later on, God modified our standards again. In the New Testament (Matthew 22:37–40), God issued two new standards: *Love God and love your neighbor.* We continuously miss the mark with those standards, too.

HOW MANY CHANCES?

How many chances should we get to follow the standards that God puts in place?

To answer that question, let's play charades. Hold up one index finger and close your fist. Yep, "God's way" has to do with one word. Now, follow that up by holding up all five fingers on one hand. Yes, you are good at this game—it's one word that has five letters in it. Hmmm...how would we act out the word? What body movements or descriptive words can you use to describe it, without using it in a sentence? You can figure that out on your own, after the word is shared...

The word is GRACE!

So, think about that for a minute – if you were playing charades, what would that look like and how would you act it out? Hmmm...

God uses grace to forgive us for the inappropriate standards we set and impose upon others. God also extends grace to us when we fail to live up to

> *God knows that we can't always load the dishwashers of our lives perfectly.*

the most appropriate standards of them all—God's standards! How does that look? Better yet, how does that feel? Ephesians 2:8–9 sums it up for us:

> *For by grace you have been saved, through faith, and this is not your own doing; it is the gift of God—not the result of works, so that no one may boast.*

God knows that we can't always load the dishwashers of our lives perfectly, nor can we make straight "As" on every one of life's tests. God understands that we will all fall short of the standards that are set for us. We get as many chances as we need because we worship a God who is above all human "standards." God gives us grace when we fail to meet the most appropriate standards that have been established for us. When we fail to live up to God's stan-

> *God wants us to love others enough to extend grace to them when they need it.*

dards, God is always there to forgive us with unconditional love. Jesus teaches the act of forgiveness to Peter using the perfect number seven and multiplying it by seventy as a standard for us to forgive others over and over as they are repentant—no count should even be taken (Matthew 18:21–22). God will do no less for us because God's love and grace is endless.

THE BEST WAY—ALWAYS "GOD'S WAY"

God does not want us to establish and use humanistic standards for personal benefit or to gain an upper hand at the expense of others with whom we live, work, and play. Instead, God wants us to love others enough to extend grace to them when they need it.

Do you think you should seek to modify your *veil of obsession* so that more grace can be extended to the others within your life?

Can you seek to be less obsessed about things of this world that do not honor God, especially your attempt to control others through unrealistic or one-sided standards that you set "your way" instead of "God's way"?

Will you unveil yourself before God and others by becoming more obsessed with seeking the most appropriate standard—to love God and love your neighbor?

Take a good look at the veil of obsession—God does!

Parting Your Veil

1. Do you practice a family tradition? What is it? Was it passed down over the years or is it something you have started?

2. What family issues do you encounter that are like the "dish war"? Do you have exceedingly high expectations of others?

3. Paul says that the body of Christ is like a human body—all the parts are important. Do you agree or disagree? Why or why not?

4. Should you seek to modify your *veil of obsession?* Do you need to offer more grace to others?

5. Will you unveil yourself before God and seek God's standards for your life?

7 ∬ Going on to Perfection

Veil of Choice

In this book's introduction, you were challenged to become aware of some of your built-in veils. As you continued reading through the chapters, you learned how to categorize your veils, figuring out that some of them can be useful to you and others are not beneficial.

As you dug in deeper, you discovered that some veils can separate you from meaningful relationships and valuable experiences. Now that you are more aware of your personal veils and you know what to do with them, we sincerely hope that your relationships have already been strengthened and your life experiences have been enhanced.

God gave us the gift of "free will" that allows us to make our own choices.

If you breezed through the introduction in an effort to get to the first chapter, you may have overlooked this simple but very significant question: *"Is there a veil that can affect your relationship with God?"*

Regardless of how you answered any of the other questions in this book, your answer to that question is the most important—the way you live out your answer may ultimately determine where you spend eternity. As you read through this last chapter, we will help you figure out whether your honest answer is a simple "yes" or "no."

CHOOSING TO SHARE

> *For everything created by God is good, and nothing is to be rejected, provided it is received with thanksgiving; for it is sanctified by God's word and by prayer (1 Timothy 4:4–5).*

As we know from this passage, everything God created is good—especially each of us. Our relationship with God is intended to be good, too. The Father, Son, and Holy Spirit desire that we share a relationship that is even more intimate than with our spouse, children, or best friends.

When God "ordered" the world and created us in God's image as rela-

We can choose to share or choose to withhold our love.

tional, moral beings, God chose to do something that is very hard for us to understand. Instead of orchestrating an element of control by completely "programming" each of us, God gave us the gift of "free will," thus allowing us to make our own choices. Therefore, we were not created as mindless puppets, but instead we were extended the grace to be unique individuals.

So, God could have arranged an evenly reciprocal and completely unveiled relationship with us, but instead, we get to choose how reciprocally unveiled we want to be. We can choose to share or choose to withhold our love with

God and/or others. In the same way, we also have the ability to choose between right and wrong. When we choose wrong over right, we sin. God allows us to sin, even though it breaks God's heart each time that we do it.

When we choose wrong over right, we sin.

Veiling our sinful choices

God did not create sin—but allows it to exist as an extension of our humanity, resulting from the gift of free will. God therefore understands and accepts that sin is a part of our imperfect human condition.

Sin became reality in the Garden of Eden where we lost our original perfection and moral character through what is known as "the Fall." Adam and Eve fell to temptation (Genesis 3:1–7). God allows us the option to veil our sin from other people, or to unveil ourselves to others through confession.

But make no mistake—we cannot veil our sins from God, even though we sometimes try.

How do we attempt to veil our sins from God? We try to do it both consciously and subconsciously. We construct and maintain some veils consciously by choosing to ignore God—by intentionally leaving our Creator out of our lives. We construct and maintain other veils subconsciously. We become so busy that we just don't think about God in the same way that God thinks about us, which is all the time.

Many scriptural stories convey God's faithfulness in always being with us. In Psalm 139 we are reminded that God knows us because God created us and is everywhere with us. In Psalm 136, we see God's steadfastness—loving humanity through difficult times, times of rejecting God, as well as times of celebration. God's love endures all things and transcends all circumstances.

Another example of God's faithfulness is in Ezekiel 34:11–16 where we see God as the Shepherd seeking his sheep, desiring to bring them into the fold regardless of where they may have wandered. God desires this type of relationship with us and continually seeks us. As Christians, we know that God desires to share in every detail of our lives, and is delighted when we choose to reciprocate in that shared relationship.

However, God does not impose himself on *every* aspect of every life. If that statement causes a blip to appear on your theological radar screen, that's great! Think about that sentence for a minute or two before you express your initial opinion on it.

> *Yes, there is a veil that can affect our relationship with God!*

A VEIL LIKE NO OTHER

So, back to that original question: *"Is there a veil that can affect your relationship with God?"* What veil could be so strong that it can affect your relationship with the One who created you, the One who sustains you and the One who loves you unconditionally? What does all of this have to do with sharing, choice, and perfection?

Enough suspense—have you figured out the answer to this simple question?

The answer is: yes.

Maybe it's more like YES! In social media, typing words in all caps is like yelling…YES, THERE IS A VEIL THAT CAN AFFECT OUR RELATIONSHIP WITH GOD! No matter how we choose to address our other veils, this veil has the power to trump them all in the end.

This veil is your *veil of choice.*

OPTIONS TO CONSIDER

As we identified and came to understand some of our other veils, we realized that we have options to consider:

- We can choose to *maintain* a veil.
- We can choose to *modify* a veil.
- We can choose to *discard* a veil.

However, with the *veil of choice,* we can also choose to *"reject."*

God knows what the word *"reject"* means and, unfortunately, God, like us, knows firsthand how it feels to be rejected.

By choosing to accept or reject God's gift of forgiveness and salvation through Jesus Christ we put ourselves on the path towards eternal consequences or eternal life. As Jesus explained:

> *"For God so loved the world that he gave his only Son, so that everyone who believes in him may not perish but may have eternal life. Indeed, God did not send the Son into the world to condemn the world, but in order that the world might be saved through him" (John 3:16–17).*

Shouldn't it be your goal to share everything with God, including eternal life—especially eternal life? If so, are your goals set correctly? Said another way, are your goals set "your way" or "God's way"?

What is your goal, as it relates to your relationship with God?

HERE'S A GOAL: ALLOW GOD TO HELP YOU MAKE CHOICES

Why do we set goals?

We are programmed through the secular influences of other people to establish all sorts of goals. The world tells us that we should set quantifiable goals to help us intentionally overcome obstacles for the purpose of reaching higher levels.

As you have tried to discern what to do with each of your veils, you may have also set a few goals along the way. You may have spent time trying to fig-

> *With the veil of choice, we can also choose to "reject."*

ure out how to maintain, modify, or discard some of your veils by consciously doing something that is measurable.

For instance, as you read through and studied the last six chapters, you may have made goals to...

...be less distracted by choosing to schedule some dream time

...overcome your complacency by choosing to pursue a new opportunity

...be less prideful by choosing to change a few of your decisions

...see past your shortsightedness by choosing to accept the help of another person or to expand your perspective

...become less self-reliant by choosing to forge a partnership with someone

...temper your obsessive nature by choosing to modify your standards

But, here's the bigger question—in all of your goal-setting, did you consciously choose to let God help you make your choices or did you veil your decision making process from God? In other words, are you setting goals "God's way" or "your way"?

The book of Galatians reminds us how God views goals. If you remember, Paul was angry and in his letter he gave the Galatians a quick lecture. At one point, he spoke directly to them about goal setting:

Are you so foolish? Having started with the Spirit, are you now trying to attain your goal by human effort? (Galatians 3:3 NIV).

We all have choices to make in life and God allows us to make them, with or without input. But aren't we like the foolish Galatians when we reach for goals without God's assistance? Sure, we can attempt to overcome many worldly milestones by setting measurable goals, but we can also be guilty of subconsciously leaving God out of many of our decisions.

Are your goals set "your way," or "God's way"?

There is one goal that we will never achieve without consciously asking for God's help: We cannot overcome sin by ourselves. No matter how hard we try or what we do, we will never achieve a goal to overcome sin on our own. However, we can choose to make it our goal to allow God to help us overcome our sin. To do this, we must fully unveil ourselves to God by asking for our sins to be forgiven.

The goal: Let God help you make choices.

Even before we took our first breaths, God had developed a plan to help us overcome our sins and even gave us a tangible example so that we could understand how it works.

GOD'S PLAN INCLUDED A CURTAIN (A VEIL)

In addition to the Genesis 3 story of the Fall, we hear again in Isaiah that man was originally separated from God by sin:

> *See, the LORD's hand is not too short to save, nor his ear too dull to hear. Rather, your iniquities have been barriers between you and your God, and your sins have hidden his face from you so that he does not hear (Isaiah 59:1–2).*

God knew that we needed help to overcome that relational separation that was referred to as a "barrier." By using the most sacred veil in all of history, God helped us to do this by revealing himself to us in a very unique way.

In Exodus 26:30–33, God instructed Moses to construct a veil in the tabernacle. No one, including Moses, really knew what the ultimate purpose of that was, but they faithfully obeyed God's command:

> *Then you shall erect the tabernacle according to the plan for it that you were shown on the mountain. You shall*

make a curtain of blue, purple, and crimson yarns, and of fine twisted linen; it shall be made with cherubim skillfully worked into it. You shall hang it on four pillars of acacia overlaid with gold, which have hooks of gold and rest on four bases of silver. You shall hang the curtain under the clasps, and bring the ark of the covenant in there, within the curtain; and the curtain shall separate for you the holy place from the most holy.

God had his own reasons for being so specific about the construction of the veil at the tabernacle. We know

The curtain was about sixty feet in height and was four inches thick.

from other biblical passages that the curtain was about sixty feet in height and was four inches thick. Even though it may have appeared to be extravagant or impractical, Moses did not question God's motivations or the specifications given for the veil. Instead, Moses was submissive to God's directive, preparing it according to the instructions that were given to him.

AFTER CONSTRUCTION—MORE INSTRUCTIONS

After the veil supports were built and the veil was hung, it was then used according to God's instructions. Only once a year was the high priest allowed to enter the Most Holy Place, also called the Holy of Holies, which was the room behind the veil. The priest was allowed to go beyond the temple's curtain for the sole purpose of offering a sacrifice on behalf of the people for the forgiveness of their sins.

This is known as the Day of Atonement (Exodus 30:1–10, Leviticus 16).

Since the people of God understood that God's presence resided in the tabernacle in the Holy of Holies, the tabernacle veil was a visible representation of the separation that existed between a sinful people and their holy God. It also was a reminder that ultimately God sets the standards for living and that those standards are so high that no human by his or her own effort can ever meet all of them, much less exceed them.

> *No matter how hard we try, we will never overcome sin on our own.*

For more than a thousand years, the structures that housed the holiest veil in the history of mankind changed in shape, form, and location. The portable tabernacle that served the Israelites during their desert wanderings eventually was replaced by the temple in Jerusalem.

The veil that hung as a reminder of the separation that existed between God and man endured every test and trial. When the temple was portable, the veil endured each move; when the temples that housed it were destroyed, it remained intact. There was a purpose for the most sacred veil in all of history—a very significant purpose, understood at first only by God!

THE PURPOSE OF GOD'S CURTAIN, UNVEILED!

As Jesus Christ was hanging on the cross, some of the people sensed that something monumental was happening, but they still did not fully realize that there was a connection between the veil and the events that were taking place. No one knew why God was so particular about that veil. To keep this all in context, we have to remember that the temple was located inside the city wall of Old Jerusalem and Jesus Christ was crucified just outside the city gate, probably within a half mile.

In Mark 15:37–38, we read the account of exactly what happened at the instant that Jesus died: *"Then Jesus gave a loud cry and breathed his last. And the curtain of the temple was torn in two, from top to bottom."* As we read the brief description of what happened on that day when Jesus gave his life as a ransom for our sins, we realize with certainty the greater purpose for God's sacred veil.

We can choose to make it our goal to allow God to help us overcome our sin.

Remember, the veil was huge (by human standards) and it was also very thick. No human could tear it; modern day studies have indicated that horses pulling from both sides could not even rip it. But the veil was effortlessly torn in half by an invisible God.

When the veil was torn, God's love was exposed to us on purpose—but what was that purpose?

BEYOND THE TORN CURTAIN

After Adam and Eve chose to sin in the garden, humanity had an inborn nature to sin, which would separate us from God. But redemption through Jesus Christ prevailed as that impenetrable veil was torn. As God intentionally discarded a separation that we had created through our choice to sin, it served as an example to all of humanity that there is one thing we cannot overcome alone, which is sin itself.

In the instant that Jesus took his last breath, God ripped apart the veil that separated a sinful people from perfection. Just as the veil endured all of humanity's tests and trials while it hung, awaiting its time to fulfill God's purpose, Jesus died for a purpose, too.

> *Our sins separated us from God, but that changed after the veil was torn.*

God did not make us perfect in the instant the veil was torn, but rather provided a way for us to eventually become perfected back into the image of God, as we were originally created. When Jesus bore our sins on the cross and was resurrected from the dead, a new covenant of forgiveness was made for ALL of God's children. This new offering of forgiveness no longer required animal sacrifices or other acts on our behalf; the death of Jesus Christ was the ultimate sacrifice. So, from the time of Jesus Christ's death and resurrection, we have been called to seek perfection, which is Jesus himself.

No matter where we are along our Christian walk, one of our biggest opportunities and also biggest challenges is to choose to accept the grace that is afforded to each of us.

The curtain was torn so that we could have a completely unobstructed relationship with God, through Jesus Christ and also so that we could experience the ultimate gift: *"For by grace you have been saved through faith, and this is not your own doing; it is the gift of God"* (Ephesians 2:8).

It is up to us to decide what we do with that gift.

VEILING OUR CHOICES

Using the example of the torn veil that once separated us from God for a purpose, let us reflect upon the veils that we have maintained in our own lives to determine if they have a purpose, too. Many of our built-in life veils have periodically protected us. But as we have grown and matured, some of our veils have outlived their initial purpose, just as the curtain of separation in the temple eventually did.

God allows you control over the veils in your life. You have the ability, with God's help, to overcome any of your veils that may be holding you back, but one of the biggest choices you will make is whether or not you will allow God to help you discern your choices.

Your *veil of choice* can separate you from…anything and everything, including God. While *God did not make us perfect in the instant the veil was torn…* God's prevenient grace continues to work throughout our lives to draw us to repentance and a restored relationship with our loving Creator, we have the freedom to choose to reject and ignore that knocking on the door of our hearts until the day we die.

GOING ON TO PERFECTION

Our sin was the reason that the ultimate veil was constructed in the tabernacle, but it was also the reason the veil was torn.

A veil no longer exists between us and God because Jesus Christ died for us. That is the ultimate Good News.

God allows us to make choices—knowing that we sin, yet still loving and accepting us. We are reminded in Romans 5:6–11 that *while we were still sinners Christ died for us.* We are further reminded that we are expected to forgive others, just as God forgives us: *"Be kind to one another, tenderhearted, forgiving one another, as God in Christ has forgiven you"* (Ephesians 4:32). This is the example by which we are supposed to live.

> *...but rather God provided a way for us to eventually become perfected.*

God will not hide our sins for us, nor will God purposefully expose them to other people. However, God forgives us through our confession and repentance, and then forgets our sins and delights in us as we continue to seek perfection along our life journeys.

We can choose to strive for perfection and even subscribe to John Wesley's doctrine that we are *"going on to perfection"* in this life. John Wesley taught and wrote that "the way to Christian perfection is best understood as an act of repentance as believers turn their backs on the sinful nature that yet remains in the heart." Wesley also taught that we can use our good judgment and wisdom to avoid whatever veils our relationship with God and seek the way to perfect love through Jesus Christ.

As Christians, we are called to *seek perfection* by seeking God in all that we do. David, speaking to his son, used these words:

> *"And you, my son Solomon, know the God of your father, and serve him with single mind and willing heart; for the*

Lord searches every mind, and understands every plan and thought. If you seek him, he will be found by you; but if you forsake him, he will abandon you forever" (1 Chronicles 28:9).

To mirror what David is asking of Solomon, have you voluntarily accepted the grace that is freely given to

God gave you control over the veils in your life.

us through Jesus Christ, who has filled the gap between our imperfections and God? And if you have, do you choose to allow God to be a part of all of your choices?

SEPARATED . . . FOR ETERNITY?

Now, let's get back to that original question . . . *Is there a veil that can affect your relationship with God?* We already answered that one—yes, your *veil of choice* can affect your relationship with God while you are here on earth. Actually, any veil that you choose to maintain between you and God can affect your relationship with God, because God desires a completely unveiled relationship with you.

As we come to the last few paragraphs of our time together, an even deeper question may be looming—what if we added the words *"for eternity"* to the original question? How would you answer it then?

*Is there a veil that can separate you from God, **for eternity?***

From Romans 8:35–39, it would appear at first glance that nothing could separate us from our Lord:

For I am convinced that neither death, nor life, nor angels, nor rulers, nor things present, nor things to come, nor powers, nor height, nor depth, nor anything else in all creation, will be able to separate us from the love of God in Christ Jesus our Lord (Romans 8:38–39).

But in Matthew 12:31–32, Jesus says,

"Therefore I tell you, people will be forgiven for every sin and blasphemy, but blasphemy against the Spirit will not be forgiven. Whoever speaks a word against the Son of Man will be forgiven, but whoever speaks against the Holy Spirit will not be forgiven, either in this age or in the age to come."

The answer to that deeper question about eternity is also "yes." As it says in Romans, nothing can separate us from the *"love of God,"* but as we learn from Jesus' words in Matthew, there is an unforgivable sin that *can* separate us from God, both on earth and after our physical deaths. The unforgiveable sin is blasphemy against the Spirit, which is also referred to as unbelief in our Lord.

> *We are expected to forgive others, just as God forgives us.*

So, it is your choice—to "reject" God by veiling yourself from the relationship that God desires, or to choose to love God as desired, by sharing all of life with God, including all of your veils.

The Veil—Torn for You

The veil at the temple was torn for each of us so that we could have both an unveiled relationship with God and the assurance of eternal life with God. However, we can choose to veil ourselves from him for eternity by rejecting God's plan of forgiveness and salvation. God desires that we strive for the perfection for which we were created. Are you "going on to perfection," or will you allow your *veil of choice* to separate you from the Father, Son, and Holy Spirit?

Are your relationships as sheer as a veil that covers a bride's face or are they opaque, like the curtain that hid the wizard of Oz from Dorothy's eyes? More importantly, have you chosen to completely unveil yourself with God?

Is there a veil that can separate you from God for eternity? Yes!

It is our prayer that we will all *"seek perfection"* each and every day. With God's help, may we all find the courage to tear through the veils of life, thus allowing God to help us live more fulfilled lives.

Eventually, as we are transformed to be eternally perfected in Jesus Christ, our veils will no longer serve any purpose; but, while we are here may we choose to honor God by living according to his example "Beyond the Torn Curtain."

Veils: Take a good look at your veil of choice—God does!

Parting Your Veil

1. What happens when we don't meet the goals we set? Read Galatians 3:3 and compare goal-setting "our way" versus goal-setting "God's way."

2. What does it mean to *"seek perfection"* here on earth? Are we "going on to perfection" as John Wesley taught we should?

3. Read Exodus 26:30–33. Why was God so particular about the instructions for the "curtain"? What what was the reason for the veil?

4. Read Mark 15:37–38. Think about the veil's thickness (4 inches) and the height (60 feet). What was the significance of its physical tearing?

5. Read 1 Chronicles 28:9. What does it mean when it says "...but if you forsake him, he will abandon you forever"? Will God really reject us forever? Now read John 3:16. What are we called to do? Do you agree with the authors that there is a veil (or many veils) that can affect our relationship with God?

6. What are the grounds for our being veiled from God for all of eternity?

7. Can the *veil of choice* cause us to stop seeking perfection?

8. With God, are you as sheer as the veil that covers a bride's face or as opaque as the curtain that hid the wizard of Oz? Or, is there any veil between you and God at all?

And all of us, with unveiled faces,
seeing the glory of the Lord
as though reflected in a mirror,
are being transformed into the same image
from one degree of glory to another;
for this comes from the Lord,
the Spirit.

2 Corinthians 3:18

About the Authors

CINDY BLOCKSIDGE currently serves as Executive Pastor at McEachern United Methodist Church in Powder Springs, Georgia. She is an ordained Deacon and has served vocationally in the local church since 1982 as a Christian Educator. She is also a licensed therapist specializing in marriage and family issues. Being both a pastor and counselor has allowed her to focus on her primary ministry calling, which is to assist people in their life and faith journeys.

Cindy resides in Kennesaw, Georgia, with her husband. Fortunately, her two grown children and their families live within the same community. Her greatest joy and favorite activity outside of the church is interacting with her five grandchildren and spending time with her family. She also enjoys being outdoors in God's creation, teaching, continually learning and sharing her gifts and blessings with others.

RANDY HARDY lives in Marietta, Georgia, with his wife and two grown sons. He is president and co-owner of a regional commercial contracting company in Marietta.

Since 1977, Randy has attended McEachern Memorial United Methodist Church in Powder Springs, Georgia. He has served on virtually every committee and teaches on a regular basis. He has been their lay leader, building committee chairman, long-range planning committee chairman, church council chairman and currently serves as the resource area lay leader.

Randy enjoys serving in the church, various outdoor activities, hunting, traveling, writing, motivational speaking, creating opportunities for other people and family time.